Praise for *The Frugal Bride*

"Who doesn't like to save money—particularly when planning a wedding? An essential resource for cutting costs without compromising the style of the wedding, this book has hundreds of great ideas and proves frugal doesn't have to mean cheap."

—CARLEY RONEY,
editor in chief, www.theknot.com

"Cynthia Muchnick helps keep both your wallet and emotions in check without compromising elegance and style. Before you say 'I do' to the florist or photographer, you should first read *The Frugal Bride* cover to cover."

—ELIZABETH ARRIGHI BORSTING,
travel writer and author,
Celebrity Weddings and Honeymoon Getaways

"Once again, Cindy focuses on providing her readers with helpful information. Now, more than ever, it makes sense to be penny-wise, and Cindy outlines smart, stylish choices."

—MARIA MCBRIDE-MELLINGER, author,
The Perfect Wedding Reception and *The Perfect Wedding*

"Who wants to start a marriage in debt? Cynthia shows us that frugal can be fun! Using these ideas you can still have the wedding of your dreams—and no one will know you saved money, too!"

—MICHELLE MERKER,
television producer/host, *Southland Today* for KDOC-TV

Also by Cynthia Muchnick

101 Ways to Pop the Question

The Best College Admission Essays

The Ultimate Wedding Idea Book:
1,001 Creative Ideas to Make Your Wedding
Fun, Romantic & Memorable

Will You Marry Me?
The World's Most Romantic Proposals

The Frugal Bride

Save Money on Your Wedding Without Losing an Ounce of the Romance

Cynthia Clumeck Muchnick

Prima Publishing

Published by Prima Publishing, Roseville, California. Member of the Crown Publishing Group, a division of Random House, Inc.

PRIMA PUBLISHING and colophon are trademarks of Random House, Inc., registered with the United States Patent and Trademark Office.

Library of Congress Cataloging-in-Publication Data
Muchnick, Cynthia.
    The frugal bride : save money on your wedding
    without losing an ounce of the romance / Cynthia Muchnick.
        p.   cm.
    Includes index.
    ISBN 0-7615-3415-6
    1. Weddings—United States—Planning. I. Cynthia Muchnick.
    II. Title.
    HQ745.M83   2002
    395.2'2—dc21   200216966

02 03 04 05 06 HH 10 9 8 7 6 5 4 3 2 1
Printed in the United States of America

First Edition

Visit us online at www.primapublishing.com

To the three joys and boys in my life:
Adam, Justin, and Jacob.
I love you all.

Contents

Acknowledgments

The Frugal Bride could not have been a success without the dedication, love, and support of many people:

•

To the hundreds of brides, mothers of brides, grooms, and wedding party guests, especially Barbara B., Sarah S., Yanina F., Kelly K., Liz N., Kim R., and many others too numerous to list who contributed their ideas to this book, I thank you.

•

To all of the hard-working staff at Prima Publishing and Random House—especially my acquisitions editor, Denise Sternad, who easily convinced me to take on another wedding project; my forever patient project editor, Michelle McCormack; and my always receptive and perky publicist, Jennifer Dougherty Hart.

•

To my friends and fellow brides: Joanne, Adena, Nancy, Mollie, Debbie, Marci G., Marci M., Holly, Lexi, Staci, Nora, Julie, Lori, Adrienne, Janine, Nikki, Haley, Colby, and Cheryl.

•

To Adam and Jen, Glenn and Lisa, Mike and Robin, Bobby and Tracy, and especially Karen and Jedd, for real-life inspiration.

•

To my creative and funky Web designer extraordinaire, Karen Gledhill (check out her brilliant work at www.cynthiamuchnick.com).

•

To Gloria, whom I couldn't live without—for your caring love and dedication to my family. You are always there. *Te quiero mucho mucho mucho.* And to Stephanie and Eric for being such special friends to my boys.

•

To those talented individuals and my esteemed colleagues who showered my work with their kind and generous words, I sincerely thank you for your praises: Connie Olson Kearns (my very own extraordinary wedding coordinator), Elizabeth Arrighi Borsting, Maria McBride-Mellenger, Michelle Merker, and Carley Roney.

•

To my relatives for your love and support: Linda, Alan, Lauren, and Evan; Karen, Danny, Benjamin, Sammy, and David; proud Grandma Lois; my e-mail pal Auntie Jill and Uncle John; my special "summer" cousins Eric, Amy, Theo, and Lucy; Gail, Andrew, Jacqueline, and Danielle; Marc, Kim, Jessica, and Blake; and Grammy Terry.

•

To Mom and Dad Muchnick for continuing to cheer me on.

•

To Mom and Dad Clumeck, for encouraging me to dare to fail gloriously and savor the passing moment; the best of times is now. And Dad, thanks for being such an amazing proofreader.

•

To Justin, may your fantastic imagination and passion for trucks, rescue heroes, and life bring you continued joy and happiness. You're my buddy, my best friend, and special gift.

•

To smiley Jake, you win me over with your warmth, good nature, and determination. I am blessed to have you as my newest son and look forward to watching you grow and become your own person.

•

And last, but certainly not least, to my patient, loving, relaxed, brilliant, handsome partner in life and crime, Adam. How can I keep writing glowing acknowledgments to you, my inspiration for it all? Without your unforgettable proposal, this entire adventure would not have culminated in this wedding, honeymoon, and amazing journey that keeps going on and on. Where has the time gone? How did we get here? You are my happily ever after. I love you always and forever.

Introduction:
Feeling Frugal and
Pinching Pennies

How many of us stop and look when we see a sale sign in a shop window? What is the attraction to the possibility of saving money? When you consider the average wedding today costs between $17,000 and $30,000, many brides are looking for more frugal ways to wed. Oftentimes, though, there is not a big red sale sign advertising vendors' discounts, nor do we see price reduction advertisements for halls, hotels, or wedding sites. Finding deals and cost-cutting strategies, however, is sometimes as easy as knowing how to negotiate and what specific questions to ask. *The Frugal Bride* will help you identify hundreds of potential wedding deals and learn how to approach them with a frugal mind-set.

Being frugal does not mean that your wedding has to look or feel cheap. Many of the most glamorous-looking touches at weddings are often surprisingly inexpensive. Additionally, some of your wedding ideas that seem financially feasible may become your most expensive elements (more on that later). First and foremost, this book will show you how to cut corners and costs without cutting out class. Couples across America have also contributed their cost-saving ideas and insights throughout the book in short quotes or anecdotal accounts.

The Frugal Bride is here for you, the bride, but also, as a bonus, special chapters in this book will assist others who are planning prenuptial parties for you. Bachelor/bachelorette parties, showers, and rehearsal dinner cost-cutting ideas are provided.

Scattered throughout the book, you'll find quick, cost-saving tips to try out when planning your day. *Frugal Freebie* sidebars are things that cost nothing to you (except maybe a bit of planning time or creative thinking). *Super Duper Deal* sidebars are cost-effective ideas. They're not completely free, but they're creative and inexpensive. *Scrimp & Save* sidebars are suggestions that save you money, but look expensive and classy so you'll never miss a thing!

Use *The Frugal Bride* as a companion to your wedding planner. You may want to read it with a highlighter pen handy so you can identify the specific areas that pertain to your event. Also, be sure to check out my other wedding book, *The Ultimate Wedding Idea Book,* for 1,001 creative, fun, and romantic wedding planning ideas.

Nowadays, planning a frugal wedding is accepted and embraced. In the twenty-first century, when more and more women and men are both in the workforce, paying off school loans, car expenses, and living expenses, brides and grooms are not as willing to blow their money on a wedding extravaganza. More couples are also financing or contributing to their wedding expenses rather than having the bride's parents foot the entire bill.

Not *all* aspects of your wedding need to be inexpensive, though. This book will help you identify the areas that you want to skimp on while saving you those extra dollars to put toward the areas that are the most important or costly for you.

I hope you enjoy the cost-cutting ideas that follow. They will help you save a bundle in planning this once-in-a-lifetime celebration of your love. Good luck pinching those pennies!

1

Being Frugal and Financing Your Wedding 101

Think of being frugal as an art form, not a science. If you are prepared and know the right questions to ask of each other and your vendors, you can shave hundreds and even thousands of dollars off your wedding expenses. Negotiating with your vendors equips you with essential ammunition you'll need to play the frugal wedding game and come out winners! Just remember: This is your wedding and regardless of what it costs or how it will be financed, you are celebrating your love.

The Bride and Groom "Money Talk"

When you consider your budget, discuss with your fiancé the elements of a wedding that mean the most to you, and then focus the bulk of your funds on those items.

•

Share your research and discuss your budget concerns.

•

Decide together to spend money on the parts of your wedding that you will really remember and cherish after it is all over. For example, the pictures will last forever, so you may not want to skimp on your photographer.

•

Set up a wedding budget on your computer with a spreadsheet or similar program. Or, go online and visit wedding Web sites (see page 191). Many provide wedding budget planners to assist you in staying within your means. Quicken or Excel spreadsheets work well, too.

Super Duper Deal

Attend local wedding expos when they come to your town or a city nearby. While the vendors can be aggressive and the crowds sometimes over-whelming, an abundance of discounts and free prizes—including honeymoons, reception sites, and limousine transportation—are raffled off.

Open up a separate checking account for your wedding expenses. It will help you keep track of your costs and separate them from your everyday expenditures.

•

Set up a wedding calendar with key dates when deposits are due, contracts need to be confirmed, and so forth. This calendar can also help you put aside the funds you need in a timely manner; perhaps a certain amount can be allotted per paycheck in the months preceding your wedding day.

•

Keep your sense of humor, as money matters can often get heated and sticky. Remind yourselves why you are getting married in the first place, and know that wedding budgeting is only the first of many financial discussions you will have for years to come. It's good practice!

Choose a day that perhaps isn't typically a "wedding" day. My husband and I were married Friday at noon at the Four Seasons Biltmore in Santa Barbara. We chose Friday simply because all the Saturdays in February were booked. But, by doing so, we were able to negotiate fees with virtually every vendor, from the officiator to the harpist. We were having a sit-down lunch at The Biltmore, which included a three-course meal (salad, entrée, and dessert plus wedding cake). Well, we didn't want dessert *and* wedding cake, so we were able to replace dessert with another course. The wedding coordinator at the hotel said this was possible because of the day we chose, and she waived the site fee for our outdoor nuptials also because we were married on a Friday.

—*Elizabeth B., Long Beach, CA*

Where Will the Money Come From?

First, review your finances together. Are you paying for your own wedding? Are parents or other relatives helping defray your costs?

•

You don't want to be poor after your wedding and blow your entire life savings on this celebration. Again, assess which areas are the most important to you, and begin shaving off other areas. For example, if having a live band as opposed to a deejay is a priority, trim the cost of your flowers or photography package. If your honeymoon is really where you want to splurge, consider an hors d'oeuvres reception only or a destination wedding (more on that later).

Decide together where you want your budget to go. We chose photography because pictures last a lifetime. That was important to me and we hired the best we could find.

—*Sarah S., New York, NY*

List your financial needs for the wedding, and formulate what you think your highest threshold of expenses will be. Then add 10 percent for a cushion!

•

See where you can cut your personal expenses prior to the wedding to save toward your big day. For instance, instead of going out to dinner and a movie for a date, eat in, rent a movie or watch one on TV, and pop your own popcorn. Put your savings from that night (and every other cheap date night) into a cookie jar or wedding bank account.

Helpful Questions to Ask Yourself

Ask yourself these questions with regard to *every* aspect of your wedding, and you'll be surprised what you may come up with.

1. What can you get donated or recycled to use as props for your wedding? For example, can you borrow silk floral arrangements or other nonperishable table centerpieces from anyone?
2. Does a friend or relative have a great car you can use as your getaway vehicle, and could that person be your chauffeur?
3. Do you know anyone with a location or home who would be willing to host your wedding ceremony or reception and by doing so eliminate your site fee?
4. Is there a dress, veil, or wedding jewelry you can borrow from a family member or friend?

Here's how we got free centerpieces. I used some old-time lanterns and lamps that my father had collected over the years from antique stores and estate auctions. We had enough for sixteen tables. For an old-fashioned touch, we sprinkled bittersweet chocolate shavings around the bases. Since we got married in a 1930s rustic lodge with exposed beams and stone, the lanterns really fit well. I would also recommend the eclectic look for people trying to cut costs. Have each table centerpiece look different—from candlesticks to plants. Cull items from neighbors, coworkers, cousins, and other friends. People are too beholden to floral arrangements as centerpieces, but a simple bowl of fruit works well and can double as the party favor, too.

—Sara S., Algona, IA

Super Duper Deal

Sign up for all free giveaways, drawings, and coupon offers at wedding retailers, registry locations, and other wedding-related vendors. Someone wins those prizes, so why can't it be you?

More Free Stuff

A small but important way to save is to see if your registries, vendors, and other wedding retailers have toll-free phone numbers, fax numbers, e-mail accounts, or addresses you can use to communicate with them. Long-distance calls and tolls can add up!

- - - - - - - - -  - - - - - - - - -

Frugal Freebie

One couple actually had their wedding sponsored by local companies and agreed to publicize items at their wedding to gain exposure for these companies. Talk about clever marketing *and* budgeting!

- - - - - - - - - - - - - - - - - - - -

The Importance of a Credit Card or Home Equity Loan

If you plan to pay for items for your wedding party such as bridesmaids' shoes or groomsmen's tuxedo deposits, use a credit card. That way, if anything goes wrong with sizes or colors, you'll have recourse through the credit card company (even if the store has a "no cancellation" or "no return" policy).

•

Use a credit card that earns you airline mileage. You may rack up enough to get free plane tickets for your honeymoon or to fly in a special guest who cannot afford the trip.

•

If you don't already have a mileage-earning credit card because of the annual fee, consider purchasing one at this time. Your $60 or so will come back to you at least tenfold in free flights.

•

If you don't have a high enough limit on a credit card to make it worthwhile to earn miles, consider getting more than one and designate it to another airline for mile-earning potential. Also, some airlines such as Alaska Air and American Airlines have reciprocity and allow for shared miles or mileage accrual to be merged to purchase tickets. Check with yours.

•

Be sure to pay off your credit card in full each month, or your interest will add up and things that were a bargain will quickly become a financial burden.

•

If you have difficulty paying off your full credit card balance, then only use the credit card for items that you may want to return or for "wedding insurance purposes."

●

Consider taking out a home equity loan. A home equity loan is a second mortgage on a residence that can be used to pay for big-ticket items such as weddings. The interest rates are not as high as those on your credit card bills, and you can often take a tax deduction on your wedding expenses if you itemize. (Ask your accountant or local bank for more details to be sure this type of loan program is right for you.)

●

If you are comfortable doing so, ask a family member for a loan to help pay for your wedding. They may offer you a no-interest or very low interest payback method.

Negotiating Techniques and Reference Checking

Are you the stronger negotiator, or is your groom? One of you should be designated in advance to take the lead.

●

Who is going to read the fine print before signing on the dotted line—you or your groom? Or, would a parent be better at reviewing these small but nonetheless important details?

•

Play your vendors' price quotes off against each other. Be careful not to use the name of the competing vendor as you may get caught in an awkward position since many know one another. The regional wedding industry is surprisingly small. However, even if you have your heart set on a particular vendor, be sure you keep a poker face to get a fair price.

•

Have your questions ready. Know what you want to ask of each vendor before your call or meeting. (Consult specific question lists in chapters pertaining to those vendors.)

•

Meet face-to-face whenever possible so you can see where your vendor conducts business. You'll quickly learn a lot about them by observing their home turf. Also, request to read reference letters and get phone numbers of couples who have used them so you can get an inside scoop.

•

Request to see a photo album or video of their work and upcoming dates of public events so you can witness their work firsthand.

Q. *Is it appropriate to ask for friends to contribute toward our home down payment or honeymoon as their wedding gift to us?*

A. Yes, it is, if that is what you truly want and it will make a difference to you financially. More and more couples are registering for nontraditional gifts as alternatives to china and dishware. Try to have some items on a traditional registry, though, so your guests can decide for themselves what they are comfortable purchasing for you.

2

The Wedding Planners and the Wedding Budgeter

An organized bride is a happy bride. Whether you are a compulsive list maker or a fly-by-the-seat-of-your-pants kind of gal, it is crucial that you implement a system of organization to help you tame the wedding beast. This tool may take some extra time to put together but will save you money in the long run since everything will be in one place. Whether you use a wedding planning book, a wedding consultant, or some combination of both, be sure you have an easy system that works for you.

Also, use some type of wedding budget planner so that you have mapped out your financial limitations and joint vision of what you plan to spend and where. Remember: Being frugal doesn't mean you have to have a cheap-looking wedding. Rather, simply assess your needs and guesstimate what your budget will be in specific areas.

The Basics of Getting Organized

First things first: Invest in a (personal at-home) wedding planner! Whether a spiral notebook, binder with dividers, or computer program, have a central system that keeps track of your estimates, expenses, and contracts. This wedding organizer will assist you in comparing price quotes and negotiating with vendors since you will be able to refer to your other bids.

●

Use something that you can carry around with you from place to place, even a laptop or other computerized organizer, so you can refer to it at all of your meetings or wedding phone calls.

The best thing I ever did for my wedding planning was go out and buy a cheap three-ring binder, dividers, and pocket pages. This tool quickly became my wedding Bible. I never left home without it, could add pages, refer to contracts, and keep everything in one, portable, centralized place. I joked to my fiancé that we should insure my binder, since it was full of such an important collection of information! This white binder housed my entire wedding brain.

—*Jennifer R., West Palm Beach, FL*

- -

Scrimp & Save

Instead of buying a published wedding planner at your local bookstore complete with checklists, question lists, and pockets, make your own. Buy a three-ring binder or accordion file, and in each section have dividers labeled with a wedding category (flowers, music, photography, etc.) and also pages with pockets where you can put receipts, contracts, coupons, business cards, and other loose items.

- -

Check out wedding Web sites (or this book's table of contents!) for other ideas on organizing your personal wedding planner. You may be able to download text to incorporate into your planner without having to buy a fancy published one.

•

Keep a list of all phone calls you have with vendors. Note the date, name of the person you spoke with, and content of your call so you can refer back to it if necessary.

•

Make copies of all correspondence—e-mail or written—and keep them in your organizer to maintain a paper trail chronicling your efforts.

•

Tear out pages from bridal publications and entertaining magazines, and download images from the Web of your dream ideas. File them in your wedding planner by topic. Perhaps something that is very expensive to execute—such as an elaborate floral arrangement—can be done more frugally by your discount florist (more on flowers in chapter 8).

Scrimp & Save

Spend time in the wedding aisle of your local library or bookstore. Read as many books as you can, and jot down ideas that excite you. Buy only the books that seem right for you, and review the chapters on budget and other money-saving ideas.

The Human Wedding Planner, a.k.a. Wedding Consultant

If you are the unorganized type, consider hiring a personal wedding planner or consultant. While this may seem like an added expense, a consultant may actually save you money by helping you negotiate and find deals within your budget.

•

Wedding consultants are a perfect link to a wide network of reputable vendors from virtually every aspect of the wedding process. After all, they would not recommend anyone who is not legitimate or professional because their job and reputation are also on the line.

•

Be sure the wedding planner you hire is quoting you a fair price. Does she charge by the hour? The event? Will she attend your rehearsal and wedding?

Frugal Freebie

Many hotels or wedding sites include their own staff wedding planner to assist you as part of their wedding package fees. This person is already paid by the hotel or site, so he or she is basically yours for free! Use this person to your advantage.

- -

Other Questions to Ask When Hiring a Consultant

1. Do you receive commissions or rebates for referring vendors?
2. Can I attend a wedding you are coordinating to watch you at work?
3. Will you be bringing an assistant to the wedding or come alone?
4. Do you take any breaks, or can I count on you for the entire duration of the event?
5. If the event goes longer than anticipated, do I need to pay you anything additional?
6. What do you plan to wear to the wedding?
7. Do you have insurance or other liability coverage?
8. What happens if you get sick or have a family emergency come up on my wedding day?
9. How have you assisted couples in saving money on their weddings? Can you clue me into your budget connections?
10. Can I see a sample of your wedding day schedule? Do you provide copies to us as well as the wedding party?

11. Will you be carrying a cell phone, pager, or other device so you can be contacted at all times by myself, the mother of the bride, or maid of honor/best man?

12. What is the average cost of weddings you coordinate?

13. Can I call some of your references?

14. What wedding day disasters have you encountered, and how have you resolved them?

15. Do you prepare a Bride's Survival Kit of essentials for any unforeseen problems or needs that occur? What is included in your kit?

16. Are you certified by the Association of Bridal Consultants (ABC)? What coursework have you taken to prepare for your job?

17. How many years have you been in business? How many weddings have you coordinated?

18. What other services can you provide to us?

19. Are you comfortable with us dictating certain things we like and deferring to you for others even if you don't personally agree with our choices? Will you be willing to step back when appropriate and be sensitive to our needs?

Not only did I save money but also my impending marriage when I fired our first wedding consultant. My fiancé did not get along with the wedding consultant we hired. He felt that she was coming between us and that she and I were ganging up on him in the wedding planning/decision-making process. She actually did begin to rub me the wrong way, too. Be sure you *both* get along with your consultant, and don't let him or her come between you. If the relationship is not working out before the wedding, you will probably be even more annoyed on the big day. Don't be afraid to offer constructive criticism or fire him or her if the relationship is not working out or what you expected.

—*Janet L., Louisville, KY*

The Wedding Budgeter

Use a spreadsheet or similar computer program to map out your best guesstimate of wedding budget and costs. Allow room to increase your numbers in certain areas and decrease in others so that you do not exceed your overall goal by 10 percent.

Frugal Freebie

Many Web sites offer free budgeters where you can input your amounts in specific areas and the program will adjust numbers to best fit into your limits. These programs are very useful if you plan to tackle things as you go or if one area costs you significantly more than anticipated and you need to cut your numbers elsewhere. (See page 191 for a listing of Web sites that offer this service.)

Many books offer ideas to break down the costs of your wedding into a comprehensive budget plan. (See page 203 for suggestions for a paper budgeter, or consult other books, Web sites, and friends for their budget systems to find the style that works best for you.)

•

You can also make up your own version of a wedding budgeter.

Time and Place

Brunches and buffets are typically less expensive than dinners or evening events.

Super Duper Deal

Have your wedding at an off-peak time of year or on an off day. June, September, and December are the most popular months for weddings, and weekends and national holidays are the most expensive days of the week to get married.

Get married in a nontraditional location such as a public school auditorium, an empty movie theater, a friend's home, or on the beach. The ceremony site fees will be significantly lower, if there is any charge at all. (Beware, though: Costs associated with the receptions at these locales may be higher than you anticipate since the cost of equipment, tables, chairs, servers, and permits may add up.)

Q. *I am the first to admit it: I am not well known for my organizing abilities. I tend to have scraps of paper with notes to myself all over the place. I'm afraid that the process of planning this wedding on my own will be too overwhelming and I might even bungle up contracts, deadlines, and so forth. What should I do?*

A. You are the perfect candidate for an at-home wedding planner as well as a human one! Buy the best published wedding planner you can find (the Beverly Clark Collection makes a nice one). Also, purchase a three-ring binder with dividers and pockets labeled for all of your wedding needs. Use this chapter for your index ideas, and also get suggestions from friends, your church, and yellow pages. Then, find yourself a wedding consultant—a worthwhile investment that in the long run will probably save you money with his or her access to vendors and other resources. Finally, stop worrying and let the fun begin with the majority of the stressful details in the hands of a professional. In fact, rent *Father of the Bride* and watch Franc, the wedding coordinator, take over.

3

Announcing Your News and Using Inexpensive Invitations

Sharing your news should not cost an arm and a leg. Neither should the paper and ink used for a wedding invitation. While some couples send out elaborate announcements of their engagement or engraved and calligraphy-scribed invitations, dozens of less expensive ways can do the job just as well.

Publicizing Your News to the World—for Free

Some magazines or papers will only print wedding announcements as opposed to engagement news. Be sure to jot those down so you can send a wedding photo and news after the fact to obtain a free public keepsake for your scrapbook.

Frugal Freebie

Contact local papers, church-affiliated bulletins, college alumni magazines or newsletters, and even your fraternity/sorority magazine to share your happy news. Often they publish weekly or monthly announcements of engagements and weddings at no cost.

Check to see if your local paper will print a picture of you two. This will also serve as a super souvenir.

Sharing the News with Family and Friends

Divide up your calling list, and have your fiancé call his friends and family.

Scrimp & Save

Some couples print up their own announcements to mail to family and friends. This approach is fine, but it can get costly with stamps, printing, and time. Calling those closest to you is an acceptable and inexpensive way to spread the news. The evening and weekend off-peak times will save on long-distance calls.

Ask your parents to contact their close friends to save you time on phone calls. Just be sure that the people they call are those you plan to have on your guest list. If you decide to have an engagement party, have those invitations serve as your announcement, too.

- - - - - - -  - - - - - - - -

Frugal Freebie

Announcing your news via e-mail is perfectly acceptable, too, and probably the most efficient. Faxing is another inexpensive alternative.

- -

Limit Your Invitees

First compile your individual lists. Then compare and discuss the invitees. Guess who will and won't attend to get a closer idea of who will actually come. This number will give you a general idea for catering costs, space needed, and other wedding aspects.

•

Consider how long it has been since you have been in contact with each individual on your list. Who would you regret not inviting versus who are you inviting because of an obligation or guilt? Remember, this is *your* wedding and *your* budget.

•

Only after you and your fiancé have your closest guess on what the responses will be, should you give your parents a number limit of guests they can invite. Have them also provide you with their guesstimate as to who they think will actually attend. Remember you are on a budget, so encourage them to stay within your limits.

Scrimp & Save

If you and your fiancé agree to limit your guest list, do not include the names of your friends' boyfriends or girlfriends on the envelopes. Some couples have an "engaged- or married-only" rule; all other guests are considered single and expected to attend alone.

Don't invite children to the wedding unless it is imperative. You'll save on costs here, too.

•

Spare yourself hassles and follow-up phone calls by assigning a number to each individual guest or family you invite. Then lightly pencil that number onto the back corner of the reply card so if a guest forgets to write their name in the space of the reply card, you can identify who they are by cross-checking the penciled number against your master list. Also, this numbering system keeps your RSVPs in numerical order so you can see who has yet to respond.

Inexpensive Invitation Ideas

Avoid the more expensive and ultratraditional style of engraved invitations, whereby the text of your invitation is literally engraved or cut into a metal plate and printed one by one. Many more cost-effective methods look just as nice, such as thermography (raised printing), laser or inkjet printing, or even handwriting.

•

Bargain shop. Select your stationery and price it at several stores, on the Web, and in mail-order catalogs. You may surprise yourself with the price discrepancies for the same or very similar item.

•

Only order the number of invitations based on the number of families and singles you plan to invite. Don't make the mistake of overordering by counting each guest as one invitation. Whether a couple, single person, or entire family, each address—not each individual—counts as one invitation. In other words, two hundred guests does not translate to two hundred invitations.

Scrimp & Save

Hand-address invitations or run the envelopes through your printer instead of hiring a calligrapher.

Negotiate with stationers. Tell them you saw the same invitations or something very similar for less. Who knows? They may give you a discount off their listed price just for asking.

•

Find a graphic designer or someone starting a printing or calligraphy business, and see if he or she will handle your printing needs to beef up a portfolio. An art student also may be interested in designing your wedding announcements and invitations as a side project for a fraction of what you would pay a stationer.

•

Purchase card stock from an office supply store, local printer, or copy shop. Then set up your invitations via computer and copy on heavy-duty photocopy machines. Mail out your invitations in the form of postcards with either a photo of you two or some other wedding image. You'll save significantly on postage, inner envelopes, and other extraneous invitation additions. The goal is simple—to disseminate information in a clear, concise way—so why not? Have them RSVP via e-mail or by phone.

Homemade Invites

Some couples design homemade invitations with photos of themselves scanned in or printed on the invitation. More and more computer programs offer creative, inexpensive alternatives to mail-order or store-bought invitations.

•

Be sure to factor in the cost of your time and what it is worth to you, because potential headaches and unforeseen costs can be associated with making your own invitations.

•

Add ribbon, tulle, or beading to your invitations yourself rather than paying a stationery company for these extras.

It was really time-consuming, but the most rewarding part of the wedding-planning process for me was making my own invitations. I have a passion for art projects, so I personally designed (with hand-tied and glue-gunned bows), printed on vellum paper, wrote, and stuffed all two hundred invitations myself. The complimentary calls and comments I received from guests were reward enough for my efforts. They were so impressed with my unique invitations and cherished the time and love that was put into crafting them. I look back on the process as my wedding gift to myself and therapy to help me maintain my sanity during the craziness of it all. And, I'd do it all over again.

—*Kiko K., Los Angeles, CA*

Another bride purchased just two reams of beautiful paper with flowers pressed in it from an office supply store. She swears that this was enough paper for all her needs: the engagement announcement, invitations, wedding programs, place cards, table numbers and thank-you cards.

•

One bride chose literally to make her own paper with construction paper, a blender, water, and flower petals. (Consult a craft store or books for more details.) Then she used tracing paper as the overlay with the invitation printed on it and attached the pages together with ribbon. The invitations were a fraction of the cost of store-bought ones and bore her personal touch, too.

If you invite a small number of guests, consider hand-writing your invitations. Forget etiquette, which dictates that you can only do that for fewer than fifty guests. You define your own rules on this one.

Cheaper Printing and Mailing

If you go the mail-order route, order invitations early—several months prior to your wedding—to avoid rush-shipping fees and to allow for any mistakes that may arise. If there are mistakes, contact the provider regarding return authorization so you do not have to pay to ship back the flawed invitations.

•

Use card stock that is a standard size. Square cards and envelopes and other oversized or odd-sized papers require additional postage.

•

Be sure the weight of your invitation and reply card does not exceed the necessity of one postage stamp so you'll save on extra postage.

•

Many lower-budget printing services will print your invitation order for much less than a stationery or wedding store will charge. Also, bridal magazines offer special reduced rates for subscribers.

Scrimp & Save

Nowadays, some couples even send their invitations via e-mail or fax. Casual can be chic and cheap! Be sure this choice fits your style, though, and note that it may offend some more traditionally minded recipients.

Announcements and thank-you cards should be ordered simultaneously to coordinate with your invitations and to avoid additional setup fees or shipping costs.

•

For thank-you cards, you can use inexpensive pre-printed cards from a stationery store (or grocery store, for that matter!) that simply say "Thank you" on the front as opposed to personalized stationery. Or, make your own cards on the computer.

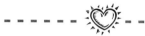

I ordered invitations from Party City, a party ware-house store. They were the same ones I saw in wedding catalogs and books, only cheaper. I also did prewedding announcements, the wedding program, the "guide to weekend activities," and others all on my computer and had them printed at Kinko's so the cost was minimal.

—*Barbara B., Newport Beach, CA*

Don't order preprinted return address envelopes for your invitations. Affix homemade labels instead.

•

Rather than feeding envelopes one by one through your computer printer to have addresses printed directly onto them, print clear adhesive address and return labels on your computer. Clear is less noticeable and a little classier than white labels, which can be distracting if your envelopes are cream or any color other than white. Print two sets of these labels so you can use them again on your thank-you note envelopes.

•

Envelopes can be handwritten or printed if you have the time. Handwriting is obviously the least expensive.

●

While some might view this as a major etiquette faux pas, if budget is your true concern, consider omitting a stamp in the reply card of your invitation and leave guests responsible for affixing their own. Or request e-mail, fax, or phone RSVPs.

●

The lighter the weight of your invitations, the less postage you will need. Eliminate extra internal envelopes, tissue inserts, or separate direction sheets. Include as much information on one card as you can.

Prewedding Information Dissemination

Save money by omitting a prewedding/save-the-date mailing to your guests. Use e-mail, word of mouth, and a wedding Web site to disseminate information. Or, set up a phone tree so your parents can call their lists and you and your fiancé can call yours with the information.

●

Postcard postage is cheaper than regular postage. Use postcards to share information that can only be delivered through "snail mail" instead of electronically.

•

Set up a wedding Web site where you can post all wedding-related information, such as where you are registered, fun photos of you two, important dates, hotel information, and locations of events. You can keep updating your site as more information becomes available. Just remember that all of your guests will not have Internet access, so be sure that those invitees get postal mailings or calls with all pertinent information.

Frugal Freebie

Many Web-hosting companies offer free wedding Web sites if you post at their location. Look into these as opposed to paying a fee to advertise your information or for a more personalized domain name. (See pertaining section on page 191.)

We created a wedding Web site that included important information on hotels, directions, activities, phone contact information, and so forth. Our goal was not to have a cheesy Web site with pictures of us and how we met. Mostly, it was a funny Web site that gave my fiancé an outlet to showcase his humor. Everyone loved it, and it was a lot of fun putting it together. As an engagement present for one of our groomsmen who was recently engaged, we set up a Web site for him and his fiancé. Domain names can be obtained for free or through many wedding Web sites at no cost.

—*Kelly B., Washington, D.C.*

- -

Q. *Help! My friend sent invitations to her guests, and some replied that their children or significant others were attending. How can I avoid that embarrassing pitfall when sending out my invites?*

A. Clearly address your envelope to only the names you plan to invite to the wedding. If you are not including children, then be sure to address the invitation only to "Mr. and Mrs." and not accidentally "The Jones Family." Also, for single guests, only write their name on the envelope. Do not add "and guest" unless you will allow them to bring someone. If you receive reply cards with additional names that you have not invited, have the person who invited them (i.e., your mother, in-laws, your fiancé, or yourself) call and explain that significant others or children are not included due to the limited guest list and size restrictions of your site or chapel. Don't be embarrassed. If they are bold enough to assume they can add others to your list or if it was a simple oversight on their part, then by all means a call to clarify is appropriate.

Wedding Party Thrift

So, you plan to honor some of your nearest and dearest friends and relatives by including them as members of your wedding party. What can you do to save? Obviously the most frugal route is to have no wedding party at all and just a witness or two at the county courthouse, but this option is not necessarily realistic for the majority of brides and grooms. This chapter describes scores of ways to save you and your attendants significant dollars while also preserving the quality and appearance of your wedding team.

General Savings

Elope and have witnesses provided by the courthouse or chapel. Another option with no attendant costs.

•

Instead of having bridesmaids, ask a few close girl-friends to help you get dressed the day of the wedding, be in charge of the guest book, do a reading in the ceremony, or serve as witness to your marriage license. They can wear their own dresses, and you are not obligated to get them gifts.

Scrimp & Save

Keep your wedding party small—maybe family only—to limit complexities and expenses related to attendants.

I had just my two sisters as matron and maid of honor at my wedding. That way I didn't have to deal with the cost and politics associated with having attendants. My stepson served as my husband's best man and also walked with him down the aisle. So the groom's attendants were his oldest best friend and his son. To honor a few close friends, I had them do readings during the ceremony but didn't have all of the bridesmaid fuss to deal with. It was just what I wanted, saving me and my groom unnecessary headaches and money!

—*Lexi K., San Francisco, CA*

Groomsmen Clothing Savings

Eliminate the tuxedo rental costs completely and allow the groomsmen to wear their own suits. Specify navy for the color since most men own at least one navy suit.

•

Add up the number of groomsmen who already own their tuxedos and let them wear their own as opposed to renting. If a few friends in your circle are getting married within the same year or two of you, see if groomsmen will buy their own tuxedos to wear to all of the functions. Owning a tuxedo can be more cost-effective than renting one more than twice in one year.

Frugal Freebie

If you do go with tuxedo rentals, let the guys wear their own black dress shoes instead of having to pay for shoes, too. No one will notice, and they will be a lot more comfortable.

Choose a tuxedo that is reasonably priced since styles all look relatively the same to your guests. Remember the idea is that the guys look the same, not that they are all in a designer label.

•

Ask the tuxedo salesperson whether he or she can cut you a deal on the quantity of tuxes you order or give the groom his rental for free since you are bringing in business.

•

Never accept the listed rental price. Always negotiate.

•

If you plan to purchase items for your wedding party such as bridesmaid's shoes or groomsmen's tuxedo deposits, pay for those on a credit card. That way, if anything goes wrong with sizes or colors, you'll have recourse through the credit card company (even if the store has a "no cancellation" or "no return" policy).

•

Remind the groomsmen to check that all of the pieces of their tuxedo are inside the garment bag before leaving the shop. It is often too late to replace items that are discovered missing on the day of the wedding. This can cost you significantly in emergency situations.

Bridesmaid Attire Bargains

Choose a specific fabric or color scheme, and send samples of it to your wedding party, so each attendant can buy or make a dress that suits her body type, style, and budget.

Super Duper Deal

Save your bridesmaids a bundle by choosing black as the color for your wedding party and letting them each wear their own black cocktail dress.

Encourage your bridesmaids to look for dresses at trunk shows, sample sales, or other discount retailers.

•

If you decide to order bridesmaid dresses through a retailer, ask the salesperson who sold you your gown about a group discount if your attendants purchase their dresses through the same store.

•

If you know someone who sews reasonably well, pick a basic pattern and some fabric and have that person make the dresses. Better yet, if it is a close friend, ask if he or she will do the sewing for you as a wedding gift.

•

Order bridesmaid dresses through a catalog. The quantity order can save you hundreds of dollars, and your attendants can have them altered slightly on their own if necessary. Plus, the catalog will send to various addresses and may waive shipping fees if you order a large quantity—be sure to ask. Also, catalog sales are generally great about returns. Check the catalog company's policy before giving your credit card number.

•

Let your bridesmaids buy their dresses off of the rack at a department store or nonwedding retail outlet. "Bridesmaid" dresses are by definition more expensive than regular cocktail dresses.

•

If the old adage, "A bridesmaid only wears her dress once," holds true, then let that truly be the case. Consider renting bridesmaid dresses from a costume, tuxedo, or prom-gown retailer.

•

If you order floor-length or an unusual-colored dress, encourage your bridesmaids to shorten or dye their dress after the wedding so they *can* get another use out of it.

Remember that having only one attendant each is very freeing. Your maid or matron of honor can select any style of dress that suits her figure, without having to accommodate any other attendants. That way she is more likely to choose something that she can wear again later.

—*Charlene W., Lakeland, FL*

Bridesmaid Beauty and Accessory Savings

Don't require your bridesmaids to wear jewelry. Or, at minimum, ask them to wear (or borrow if they don't own) pearl or diamondlike stud earrings. Less can be more and will save everyone money!

•

Allow your bridesmaids to wear their own black or white heels instead of insisting they dye shoes to match their dresses. Or, select a basic shoe for them from a discount shoe store that they will be able to wear again after the wedding.

•

If the wedding is outdoors or takes place during a warmer season, don't require your attendants to wear expensive pantyhose. If you do require hose, purchase them for your attendants at a discounter. Collect their sizes so they can all be bought at the same time and are the same brand and sheerness. (Purchase a few extra pairs in case of runs or snags!)

•

Don't buy pantyhose with beading, lacey frills, or other unique touches. Keep them plain and simple (i.e., inexpensive).

•

Skip accessories like shoe clips, ornate jewelry, shawls, hair bows, and other unnecessary frills that will add to your attendant cost but not make a great difference to their appearance. Simple is better and less expensive!

Scrimp & Save

Find a dress that allows your attendants to wear their own regular bras (as opposed to expensive corsets or strapless bras that they may only wear once). If they do need to wear a special type of lingerie, encourage them to borrow.

Have bridesmaids do their own hair rather than paying for a group salon session before the wedding. Or, if you personally know a good hair and makeup person, see if he or she will do it for your group as your wedding gift.

•

Encourage bridesmaids to get manicures before they arrive (simple French or pale polish so they all look the same). Their own manicurist will definitely be cheaper than the hotel's, if that is your wedding site. Plus, you won't feel obligated to treat them to manicures if you do a girls' salon morning the day of the wedding.

Frugal Freebie

Send your bridesmaids to a department store to have their makeup done for free the morning of your wedding. Preselect what brand you want them to use as well as eye shadow, lipstick, and liner colors. Then buy one lipstick for them to share for touch-ups throughout the photos and the actual event.

- -

Ring Bearer, Flower Girls, and Junior Bridesmaid Cost-Cutting Tips

Have someone make the ring pillow for a fraction of the cost of purchasing a premade one. Create it with hand-kerchiefs or even a pillowcase, and add some lace or extra dress fabric from your gown or bridesmaid dresses. Fill the pillow with stuffing or scented pot-pourri.

●

Do as one bride did and borrow a ring pillow from a married friend. It will be as good as new since it has only been used once!

●

Instead of purchasing, rent the ring bearer outfit from a tuxedo shop.

•

Advise the ring bearer's parents to check resale shops or children's apparel consignment stores for formal outfits. Many for resale have only been worn once, especially children's dress shoes.

•

Have a family friend make the ring bearer's outfit with a small color-coordinated touch such as a pocket handkerchief, tie, or a colored accent pillow that matches the wedding party colors.

•

Allow the ring bearer to wear simple slacks or shorts, oxford shirt, and vest or blazer. Remind the mother of the ring bearer that these items can be borrowed or rented.

I borrowed a ring bearer outfit for my son from a girlfriend whose son had been in a wedding a few weekends earlier. I used masking tape to "hem" the pants and stuffed tissue in the toes of the shoes. It worked out just fine and saved me the cost of renting or buying a child's tuxedo! The bride also had my son carry the ring pillow that was carried at my wedding and used that as her "something borrowed."

— *Cindy C., Ross, CA*

Have the parents of your flower girl or junior bridesmaid select a plain white or color-coordinated dress that they already have or can rent for the wedding. Don't ask them to go to the expense of having a dress made for the one-time walk down the aisle.

•

Christening or Easter dresses work well for flower girls who can later use the outfit for playing dress-up! Purchase them after the Easter holiday to find sale prices.

•

Off the rack will be cheaper than buying a "flower girl" dress.

•

Designate a junior bridesmaid from the rest of the wedding party with a special sash, scarf, or different floral arrangement rather than having an entirely separately styled dress.

•

If your attendants' dresses are not too revealing, just order the same dress in a smaller size for the junior bridesmaid.

•

Or, have a junior bridesmaid select a dress in the same color as your wedding party but a more suitable style for a younger girl. Perhaps another dress in your color group or fabric selection would work.

Bargain Gifts
for the Wedding Party

Consider earrings or other costume jewelry that you want the bridesmaids to wear for the ceremony, an inexpensive stationery set (monogrammed or not depending on budget), a picture frame with a quote in it, or small, pretty handbags to use at the wedding.

I had a friend in the printing business who printed up personalized stationery sets for each of our male and female wedding attendants. He gave us the stationery as our wedding gift—along with enough for us to write our thank-you notes on. He saved us from having to buy gifts for our wedding party and thank-you cards for ourselves!

—*Ken G., St. Louis, MO*

A new inexpensive trend is to give wedding party gifts that grow, such as perennial flowers (or seeds) that will bloom each year to remind attendants of your special day. Attach a simple card with a note explaining why you have selected this sort of thank-you.

●

For groomsmen, purchase inexpensive group sales tickets to a sports event—even if you are sitting in bleachers or high-up seats. You can attend the event together over the wedding weekend, and the outing makes a fun, unique gift idea that you can share.

●

For bridesmaids, pamper them with a spa certificate—maybe you can arrange for a price break if you go as a group! Or, go together to a massage school where students are training to give massages for a fraction of the cost.

●

If your event is not black tie, purchase color-coordinated ties for your groomsmen as their gifts.

●

Print up wedding weekend T-shirts at a local copy shop with the date, your names, and even a scanned picture of yourselves as a fun and inexpensive memento.

Scrimp & Save

Make gifts using items from craft stores, computerized programs, or your own artistic talent.

Give the wedding party a special bottle of wine labeled with your own message (use a metallic pen or computerized label). Once they drink the wine, the bottle serves as a nice souvenir. Purchase the wine by the case or from a wholesaler or warehouse store to get the best price.

•

Decorate inexpensive plastic or wooden picture frames with paint pens, glitter, lace, or other trinkets from craft stores. Insert a preprinted message in the frames and after the wedding mail your bridesmaids and groomsmen a photo from the wedding to place in it.

•

A ceramic mug full of jelly beans, chocolate kisses, M&Ms, or other tasty treats makes a nice souvenir and thoughtful memento.

•

Head to a local discount warehouse such as Costco or Sam's Club for off-the-beaten-path items like fun beach towels, home accessories, flowering plants, thematic DVDs or videos (*Four Weddings and a Funeral* or *Father of the Bride*) CDs, or other appropriate items on sale at quantity discounted prices.

•

Gift certificates for the following work for both genders: movies, theater events, music stores, coffeehouses, restaurants, or video rentals. Even a phone card with long-distance minutes would be thoughtful and appreciated!

•

Search for deals at outlet shopping malls. Scarves, small leather goods, travel items, or lingerie are all fun items to get for bridesmaids. Wallets, business card holders, travel kits, neckties, or key chains are excellent ideas for men.

Q. *I am struggling to select my wedding party and don't want to hurt any feelings of others who have included me as an attendant in their wedding. I cannot pare down my choices and am already up to twelve brides-maids! What should I do?*

A. Don't feel that you have to include those who have included you unless they are truly your nearest and dearest friends and your party will not feel complete without them. Imagine who you will be close to in twenty years and start eliminating from there. If feelings are hurt, so be it. This is your wedding day, and too large a wedding party adds up in costs and complexities. Instead, consider bestowing other duties such as reading a poem or passage during your ceremony, serving as witness to your marriage certificate, or being in charge of your guest book.

Registry Tips to Save You (and Your Guests) Money

Registering can be a sticky process. You want to get great gifts and things that you and your partner need for your new life together, but also you may want to do some out-of-the-ordinary things with contributions to help defray wedding, honeymoon, or new-home costs. Read on to find out how you can gain and save for yourselves and even your guests.

Why Register?

Some couples feel awkward or strange selecting gifts. If this is the case for you, think of registering as a service you are providing for family and friends as well as for yourselves.

•

As a couple, you know the most about what you like and need, and registering allows guests to choose an item from your list that fits into their budget and is the particular type of gift they want to give you.

•

Registering will save you a huge amount of time, effort, and money by limiting your need to return or exchange items that do not appeal to you or that you already have.

•

Think of registering as a shopping spree without a cash register at the end!

Choosing Stores
with Frugality in Mind

Check stores' customer service, return and exchange policies, and accessibility for your guests who live in other parts of the country and world. Some stores, for example, offer only store credit for gifts you return, while others give cash refunds, which you may prefer. Other stores have a time limit for returns.

•

Be aware that some department stores insist on gift receipts for returns; others only offer you the most recent sale price within the last thirty days for a returned item without a gift receipt. This can be problematic, so be sure to ask the stores about these issues prior to establishing your registry.

•

Think of registering at stores beyond the traditional houseware retailers or department stores. Home improvement, sporting goods (Recreational Equipment, Inc. (REI)), discount (e.g., Target, Bed, Bath & Beyond, IKEA), entertainment equipment, and many others offer registries.

My fiancé and I are avid hikers and enjoy the great outdoors. We decided to register at REI (Recreational Equipment, Inc.) for nontraditional items like a tent, rappelling ropes, and other hiking and camping gear. We received just what we wanted!

—*Robin F., San Francisco, CA*

New Trends in Fiscally Minded Registering

Some couples register for items beyond the traditional china, crystal, silver, appliances, and cookware. Instead, they opt for more practical, homeowner-oriented items such as furniture, barbecue grills, televisions, sporting goods, camping equipment, artwork, and even computers.

•

You may want to register for towels, bedding, napkins, or tablecloths, too, to save yourself that expense.

Frugal Freebie

Many couples today register at travel agencies or mortgage lenders to allow invitees to contribute toward their honeymoon or home down payment. If you choose this type of registry, though, be sure that you also have a separate registry for more traditional wedding items so guests have a gift option other than a cash contribution.

If you don't have a great luggage set, register for one. You'll enjoy it on your honeymoon, future travels, and business trips.

•

Register for a season subscription or individual tickets to the theater, symphony, or opera. This is the type of splurge that you may not choose to spring for when you are married and will thoroughly enjoy if it is pre-arranged and paid for by someone else!

•

Register for membership to a health club or renewal of your current membership.

•

Register for classes you can take alone or together after you are married such as cooking, dance, computer, or athletic classes such as yoga, Pilates, or aerobics.

•

Philanthropic brides and grooms may request that in lieu of a gift guests give donations to selected charities that mean a great deal to the couple personally in lieu of a gift. This type of registering is more common in second or third marriages in which couples already have many of the home items that they need.

Frugal Freebie

Spread the word that frequent flyer miles, hotel accommodations, or Eurail train passes (if you honeymoon in Europe) would be appreciated as a gift. One of your guests may have a connection to some of these more obscure items on your wish list.

Registering for China

Even if you two don't think you'll be entertaining formally for many years, this is the time to acquire your
china. After all, do you think you'll go out and buy
china for each other on your tenth anniversary?

•

The same goes for crystal and silver flatware. However,
keep in mind that if you don't think many of your invitees will be able to afford these higher-priced items, you
may want to use your store credits from returned gifts
toward completing these sets.

•

Many everyday stemware and flatware items can be
mixed in with your formal china, which will save your
guests money and also eliminate the need for you to
have totally separate full sets for everyday and fine
china.

•

Registering for a set of all-white dishes or a simple pattern, such as a white dish with single gold or blue band
around the edge, can be a great way to get the best of
both worlds. You can mix in any bowls, salad plates,
and table linens more easily, and the dishes will never
go out of style.

•

See if the retailer where you register offers discounts to you after your wedding date to assist you in purchasing any remaining pieces in your china pattern that were not filled.

•

Consider registering through Michael C. Fina, Ross Simons, or other reputable gift catalogs that offer significant discounts on hundreds of china patterns, silver, flatware, glassware, and other wedding-related items. (See pertaining section on page 197 for more contact information.)

Financial Tips on Registering

Be sure to select gifts in a wide range of prices.

•

Use in-store registry checklists to help you consider all that you need. Be cautious, though: Since stores want you to register for a lot of things, their checklists may include some extraneous items that you don't really need.

We registered for six sets of crystal $100 candlesticks. The price point seemed good for our guests. We only ended up keeping one set and used the balancing $500 credit toward more expensive items to complete our silver flatware. It worked out great, and now six families think they gave us the candlesticks, which we love, by the way, and proudly display.

—*Wendy S., Jackson Hole, WY*

Use common sense. Do you really need an ice cream maker, fondue pot, or bread machine that you may only use only a few times, as opposed to more practical (but less exciting) items that you will use every day, such as measuring cups, bowls, and glassware?

•

Higher-priced gifts are ideal for a group of family members, friends, your wedding party, or coworkers to chip in on together.

Registry Money Matters

Set up a wedding account for you and your fiancé for checks of congratulations that may arrive after your engagement.

•

Many guests bring checks in cards when they come to your wedding. Be sure to have your maid of honor or best man keep these for you during the event. Some couples even have a small fabric bag or box to collect cards with checks enclosed.

•

Any store credit that you receive on returns should be spent relatively quickly, especially if the store is a small, nonchain retailer. You won't want the store to go out of business before you have a chance to exchange your items.

•

Keep a master list of all gifts received, and list the approximate cost of the gift so you know how to reciprocate at a future occasion or celebration in their honor.

•

Finally, if the wedding is canceled, you should return all gifts received.

Q. *My fiancé feels uncomfortable registering. He thinks it is presumptuous, tacky, and greedy. How can I convince him it's acceptable?*

A. Spell it out for him if you have to! Registering is the best way to ensure you get what you want to start your new life together. Not only is it *not* considered tacky, it is a tradition and your guests come to expect it from brides and grooms—and every other wedding they attend. Choosing what you want eliminates the need for time-consuming returning of gifts that don't appeal to you or are extraneous. Also, registering allows you to determine what your needs are as a couple. Your guests will be inconvenienced if there is no registry spelling out what your tastes and needs are. If he still feels uncomfortable with this form of registering, maybe he is the unconventional type who would prefer to have guests contribute to your home down payment fund or honeymoon. More and more couples are opting for this new idea.

6

Prenuptial Party Penny-Pinching

Parties and showers will be held to celebrate your impending union. How can you assist your party givers in saving a buck or two? There are many ways to cut corners and costs without cutting out class. Read on to find out more.

Showers on a Shoestring

Have the event at the home of one of the shower hosts.
A potluck dinner or one cooked by the hosts and bridesmaids might fit into their budget.

●

Consider a couples shower. This is becoming increasingly popular as opposed to the "girls only" tradition.
You can also save by combining the shower festivities
with the bachelor/bachelorette party and celebrate the
events all at once.

Scrimp & Save

Have a potluck shower where each guest is assigned to bring food and beverages.

Budget Shower Touches

Consider using potted plants, confetti, or balloons as
centerpieces instead of elaborate flower bouquets.

Scrimp & Save

Make homemade, edible favors such as cookies or fudge.

Other cute, inexpensive shower party favors include small plants, sachets, scented soaps, candles or bath oils, a decorated tin full of colored jelly beans or pastel-colored candies, tiny glass vases with fresh-cut flowers, homemade brownies or pretty cookies wrapped in colorful cellophane and ribbon, a box of festive tea bags or coffees, miniature books, picture frames, stationery, and pretty notepads.

•

Supply free entertainment. Guests can bring anecdotes about you, compete to dress you in a toilet paper gown, or take trivia quizzes about you and the groom.

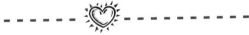

If one or more groups of friends are giving you a shower or engagement party, see about consolidating decorations. Concentrate on purchasing centerpieces, banners, tablecloths, and so forth, that can be used for the showers, parties, and reception. It's like getting things half or two-thirds off. Avoid items such as crepe paper or balloons that will not hold up from one event to the other. If you are having different showers with different groups of friends at each one, few would notice a repeat of decorations.

—*Charlene W., Lakeland, FL*

- -

Frugal Freebie

Play board games for entertainment: Pictionary, Scattergories, bridge, poker, or charades are fun choices. The more interactive and team-oriented the game, the better!

- -

Rent a karaoke machine for hours of embarrassment and singing fun. Videotape the singers!

•

Inexpensive door prizes or gag gifts are a good incentive to break the ice and get people into the swing of things.

•

Have one of your bridesmaids collect the ribbons off of your shower gifts and insert them into a paper plate or box top. That way, you'll have a great souvenir and free bouquet to practice with at your wedding rehearsal.

•

Finally, a note to the bride: Of course you will write a thank-you note, but don't forget to bring a gift for the hosts of your shower to show your gratitude. A plant, cut flowers, wine, and homemade fruit basket or cookie bouquet are inexpensive ideas.

Budget Bachelor/ Bachelorette Parties

Economical Locations and Activities

Consider some of these fun and less costly locations: a spa or golf club weekend getaway (hopefully someone is a member and can get you a complimentary room or discounted rates); a winery that offers free tours and tastings; a live sporting event (seat location doesn't matter!); a weekend at a beach house or ski lodge (which belongs to someone you know or who can get you a price break); a retro disco dancing place; a karaoke or dueling piano bar; a sports bar; a western theme bar with electric bull and line dancing; a funky, new restaurant; a comedy club (be sure to let them know who the bachelor/bachelorette is so they can be razzed!); or a ceramics-painting studio where partygoers can drink wine and decorate items for the couple's new home.

My maid of honor brought me to a dueling piano bar, tipped the pianists, and had me go up on stage to be serenaded in front of everyone. I also had to do a shot with my hands behind my back. It was fun, harmless razzing and not as costly or raunchy as going to a strip bar. We all sang songs until dawn!

—Colby M., Fullerton, CA

Microbreweries can be rented out for groups to brew and bottle their own beer. Some establishments even have personalized computer label-making capabilities, so the bride and groom's names and wedding date can be printed on the bottles. Free samples are also available at some microbreweries if you choose simply to visit instead of renting out the place.

●

If you have a co-ed bachelor/bachelorette party, the group can celebrate together by playing a co-ed softball game or a round robin volleyball tournament, renting a boat and hanging out on the water, having a beach barbecue, joining in a men versus women scavenger hunt, or another fun group event that doesn't cost too much.

•

Bring a disposable camera on your night out to record the highlights of your evening. Later on, write captions on the pictures to chronicle the activities, and put them in an inexpensive album to keep as a memento.

•

A scavenger hunt is also an inexpensive activity. You or the groom can pose for pictures with members of the opposite sex you encounter throughout the evening. You and the groom can be required to collect risqué things from these folks such as an article of clothing, a kiss on the cheek, or an autograph.

Super Duper Deal

Have an ice cream sundae social or pizza-making party. Good eats and making things together make for great ice breakers and memories.

Economy-Priced Attire and Fun

You and the groom can dress in a way that distinguishes you from the rest of the group—a headband with white fabric attached to represent a wedding veil for you, a "groom" sign hung around the neck of the groom, or a baseball cap emblazoned with "bride" or "groom" will do!

•

Dress up with a cheap necklace from a gumball machine and, throughout the evening, have men bite off one candy at a time. Photograph these moments.

Super Duper Deal

One group of bridesmaids baked a cake shaped like male genitalia to eat at the party. It makes for great photo opportunities and funny memories.

Dirty magazines, videos, or funny sex toys are much less expensive than hiring a stripper and also less potentially harmful to you, the groom, or a raucous group of revelers.

•

Chip in on cab fare or a responsible designated driver to chauffeur you throughout the night.

Reasonable Rehearsal Dinner Themes and Locations

Plan a theme for the rehearsal dinner and weave it throughout your centerpieces, attire, or entertainment. Then hunt for deals that reflect the budget. One couple had all the guests arrive in western garb for their hoe-down barbecue rehearsal dinner complete with hay bales and square dancing, while another served up make-your-own-fajitas at a Mexican fiesta.

•

Better yet, forego the centerpieces, decorations, and other extraneous elements entirely.

•

Consider alternative locations for the rehearsal dinner such as the back room at a fun pizza restaurant (which can be reserved for free!), a beach cookout, or a public park where you can barbecue.

Inexpensive Personal Touches and Decor

Many of the following ideas can apply to both the rehearsal dinner and the wedding reception.

•

Put together a "slide show" on a laptop computer with scanned-in photos (as opposed to organizing and paying for a video or slide show presentation) chronicling your relationship. Then play it on a projector.

•

Have photos of you as babies or as a couple enlarged to poster size at your local printer or copymat and hang them as decoration. You can transform a black-and-white photo reprint from a photograph to an eleven by fourteen-inch poster on a copy machine for under a dollar, and it looks as good as a professional photo enlargement.

•

Make several posters with photos or a collage of you and your fiancé with your friends and relatives. Put small captions beneath the photos so the wedding guests can find themselves and remember the fun times you have shared.

Frugal Freebie

For minimal cost, put together a photo album or scrapbook of your relationship for guests to peruse.

Make a poster-board time line of your lives and relationship with short descriptions of significant dates and events such as when and where you were born, where you attended college, how you met, where you shared your first kiss, and how you or the groom proposed.

Frugal Freebie

Collect and label photos of your parents, grandparents, siblings, and fiancé's family's weddings and share them on a display table.

Q. *Is having just a couple's shower enough for the bride and groom, or should the bride have an additional shower of her own?*

A. One shower is plenty for a couple getting married and may save money by combining the events and having a group celebration. Plus, the event may even be able to double as a bachelor/bachelorette party, if the couple does not feel the need to have these prenuptial events, too. Fun themes that both genders will appreciate are "Around the House," for which each guest brings a gift that corresponds to a preassigned room of the house, or "Outdoor Activities," for which guests bring items such as sporting equipment, beach towels, or exercise gear. The "Handy Couple" shower is also popular for the honorees to stock up on tools and home accessories, and "That's Entertainment" is a fun theme for stereo or video equipment, CDs and videos, and maybe even a popcorn popper.

Cost-Effective Ceremony Sites and Other Bargain Places to Wed

The traditional chapel and reception hall or hotel wedding with all of the trimmings can average from $17,000 to $30,000 (in larger cities). Of course, no couple wants to return from their honeymoon to heaps of debt. Why not try some less traditional but increasingly popular alternatives to the standard wedding? Read on to find some creative bargain ideas for wedding locations you may not have considered.

Date and Site Selection Strategies

Make booking your site one of the first things you do so you can lock in dates and times. Have a few alternative choices ready.

•

If you find a site you like that fits into your price range and overall checklist, book it! Even if it is not your first choice, if it is available on your selected date and comes with a refundable deposit fee, grab it before someone else does.

Frugal Freebie

Think hard about people you know who may have contacts at a large home, ranch, garden, or other private location and would be willing to host your event without a site fee.

Have your ceremony and reception at the same location so that you can reuse chairs, tables, flowers, and other décor from the ceremony at the reception.

●

If you get married at a church or other religious location, plan to have your reception there, too, since religious halls are usually less costly than hotels.

●

Get married on a nonholiday weekend, on a weekday, or at another off-peak time. Consult the specific location to find out when these are. The most common off-peak months to wed are between November 1 and April 30 (December tends to be pricier due to the holidays, though). June and September are the most popular months for weddings, while Saturday nights and Sundays of national holiday weekends are typically the most expensive days of the week.

●

When picking an economical date and location, consider Thursday, Friday, or Sunday evenings. Better yet, brunches or weekdays are less costly if your schedule permits.

●

Be flexible regarding possible dates and times at more unusual locations.

Frugal Freebie

Dig deeply into your contact list to see if anyone you know works for or can get you a deal on a hotel location for your wedding. You may be able to get a site or room fee waived if you meet the hotel's guest number quota or agree to do all of your catering in-house.

If you find that your possible dates are costing too much, ask vendors what their off-peak times are so they'll be motivated to lower their prices for you.

•

Take advantage of the times of year when daylight savings kicks in, especially if you are conducting an outdoor event. That extra hour of daylight could save you in your overall costs, especially if you plan to rent heating lamps, supplemental lighting, and other outdoor amenities. Bands, caterers, and photographers often reduce their rates significantly for daytime events, too.

•

Find out what extras your reception site is willing to throw in as perks if you choose them over their competitors—for example, free corkage, complimentary cake slicing, overtime at the open bar, free nonalcoholic beverages, or their own mode of transportation such as a limousine or town car at no charge. Also, some locations will provide flowers, tables and linens, and other decorative touches for the asking.

- - - - - - - - -  - - - - - - - - -

Frugal Freebie

Some hotel locales offer a free honeymoon suite as well as rooms in which the wedding party can get ready for the ceremony.

- -

Don't be afraid to ask for a lower price than you are initially quoted, especially at the location that is your first choice. You may be pleasantly surprised that vendors will negotiate with you or, at minimum, throw in more free extras to defray other costs. Speaking up can save you hundreds!

●

If you book your location far in advance, get assurance in writing that the vendor will lock in the price you were originally quoted. That way, if there is a price increase, you'll only be responsible for what you originally agreed to pay.

•

Get everything in writing, especially items you negotiate that are outside the boilerplate contractual language!

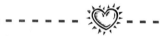

We met with several large hotels, and I sort of bat-
tled them against each other, telling one that the
other had offered to throw in this or that or do
things a certain way. By negotiating and playing
the hotels off against each other, I was able to get
the one I preferred to lower their prices. Since we
had planned a large wedding with over 400
guests, we reserved sixty-five hotel rooms for the
weekend and also hosted two brunches with over
150 guests. Then I returned to the other location
and told them what was being included by their
competition. The new location comped us a few
more perks to seal the deal, such as waiving the
cake-cutting fee, an open bar for one-and-a-half
hours for the same price as one hour, and unlim-
ited wine free of charge.

—*Barbara B., Irvine, CA*

Off-the-Beaten-Path Ceremony Sites

Considering the number of guests, start to brainstorm alternative ceremony sites that would accommodate your group.

•

Consult local travel books, wedding publications, yellow pages, and even the area's Chamber of Commerce for ideas on free or almost free ceremony sites. A public museum, park, beach, zoo, aquarium, historic home, college or university campus, school auditorium, movie theater, community center, garden, library, or even theme park are all creative alternatives and potential bargains.

My mother knew someone who had a ranch just outside Los Angeles. This person gave us the use of their location as a wedding gift, even though they usually charge to rent it out for special events. They already had chairs, a dance floor area, tables, and even a sound system that we were able to borrow for our event. It was a unique space that accommodated a large group, and because of the personal contact, we were able to use their resources and references for catering at a discount.

—*Matt B., Los Angeles, CA*

- -

Virtually any location can host a wedding. Just be sure to look into any permit requirements, which will still probably cost much less than reserving a large hotel or banquet hall.

•

Bed and breakfasts, historic homes, or inns are often less costly alternatives and more quaint than larger, big-name hotels.

•

Have an outdoor wedding if climate will allow. Daytime ceremonies and receptions will also eliminate the costs associated with renting tents, heating lamps, and supplemental lighting.

•

Find out if these locations have an on-site coordinator who can assist you with logistical details associated with that locale (e.g., table and chair rentals, catering concerns, etc.).

•

Check to see if any other weddings are taking place at your location on the same day. Perhaps the other wedding couple would be interested in sharing costs of items such as flowers, music, chair, and table rentals.

•

Look into neighborhood clubhouses, which usually charge a nominal fee or only a refundable damage deposit and have ample parking for a small to medium-sized reception. These clubhouses often overlook a pool or grassy area and only require that you are connected in some way to a homeowner who will be responsible if there are damages.

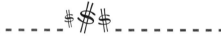

Scrimp & Save

Many fraternal organizations such as Elks or Rotary Clubs have halls where they conduct events and regional meetings. If you know or, better yet, are related to a member, that person can sponsor your wedding or reception and may even waive site fees.

Getting Married Abroad and Destination Weddings

For couples paying for their own weddings, destination weddings cost about one-third the price of traditional weddings.

•

Destination weddings are intimate and cost-effective, since they tend to involve fewer guests and eliminate transportation costs to your honeymoon (because you're already there!).

•

The guest list for your destination wedding can be as short or long as you choose. You two can be the only attendees, and the hotel coordinator can provide you with witnesses, or you can have as many people as you like who are willing to fly to your destination.

Destination Wedding Hotel Perks

Check with the hotel at which you plan to wed for pricing on different wedding packages. The prices range greatly as you add on different perks to your ceremony and reception.

•

The wedding specialists at hotel properties can also arrange for beachside, cliff top, boat, or even hot air balloon locations. One couple in Hawaii exchanged vows atop donkeys at the peak of a volcano. For such a unique locale, they paid significantly less than they would have had they gone for a traditional wedding with all of the trimmings.

Frugal Freebie

Many hotels offer destination wedding packages that include free nights for the bridal couple as well as discounts to wedding guests staying at the hotel.

Where to Have a Destination Wedding

If you want to get married in Paris, Venice, aboard a pirate ship, or other exciting locales but want to skip the passport and expense, Las Vegas has gone way beyond spur-of-the-moment elopements. Every theme hotel offers unique packages from the traditional to the adventurous. Say "I do" atop a replica of the Eiffel Tower at Paris, aboard a pirate ship at Treasure Island or a gondola at The Venetian, in a Renaissance ceremony at The Excalibur, in a replica of Elvis's Graceland Chapel with an Elvis impersonator as your minister, or many others. Contact hotels directly or the Las Vegas Tourism Office for more information.

•

Get married for free with the basic Sandals Weddingmoons package at most Sandals resorts (www.sandals.com or 1-888-SANDALS). Leave your worries behind and let the staff plan every detail while you just show up and enjoy.

•

Other all-inclusive hotel chains offer special packages for couples who get married at their resort. Consult your travel agent or the property directly for more information.

Scrimp & Save

If you two feel that off the wall or simple is for you, then elope to Las Vegas, the world's wedding capital; or stay local and visit your justice of the peace or courthouse.

Carnival Cruise Lines offers complete wedding packages with all of the trimmings. Guests can attend the ceremony and reception while the ship is at the port, and as the ship sails, the couple is off for their honeymoon! What a fun alternative to the traditional limousine exit. Check into this and other cruise lines to handle all of the details for a fraction of the cost of a traditional wedding.

•

Other than exotic islands or faraway places, unique locations for destination weddings or receptions include a winery, farm, art museum, sculpture garden, university quadrangle or church of your alma mater, atop a building or skyscraper, a historical landmark, race track, ski slopes, basketball court, botanical gardens or lakeside, movie studio or theater, or at your own or close relative's home (more on that in the next section).

Getting Married at Home

Benefits of Home Weddings

Exchanging your vows at a home can have a more intimate and special feel than getting married in a church or hotel. The symbolic nature of beginning your lives together in a home environment can be deeply meaningful and personal.

•

Homes can also host just the reception after a church ceremony. This choice may work out to be easier than hosting all at one location but may not be convenient in terms of the physical distance between the ceremony and reception.

Frugal Freebie

Home sites can serve as an all-inclusive locale: the ceremony, cocktail, and reception site all rolled up into one—for no site fee!

Homes offer elements of comfort that other locales cannot. You can get ready prior to the ceremony in a home setting, have a quiet place (that is not a hotel room or public bathroom) where you can retire for a few moments to regroup, and you'll also benefit from other small comforts like having a refrigerator, television, personal bathroom, and phone line.

I was married at my parents' home. We were able to use all of the chairs, flowers, and same staff people to assist from the ceremony through the cocktail hour and until the end of the evening. Therefore, we saved on transportation costs and extra flowers and got our money's worth on rented items and staff help. All guests stayed at one location, and a good time was had by all.

—*Cindy C., Kentfield, CA*

A Few More Home Wedding Tips

If you plan an at-home wedding at your or the groom's home or at the home of your parents or in-laws, it is a good idea to hire a wedding coordinator to assist with the hundreds of unforeseen complications that may arise.

•

Don't feel the need to be excessive in decorations by adorning the garden or trees with ribbons, fabric, or extra accessories. Let the beauty of the outdoors be just that: natural beauty. As soon as you pick the home site, begin to plant or add to the existing garden in anticipation of the wedding event.

Scrimp & Save

Try to reuse the chairs from your ceremony again at the reception as well as any floral arrangements that you may have. This recycling requires help in transporting these items, but may be more cost-effective.

Q   *My friend's father collects antique cars and has offered the use of his "garage" warehouse as a unique wedding location. The location is free, but what concerns should I have about other areas of cost?*

A.   What a wonderful opportunity. However, there are a number of other costs to consider: table, chair, and linen rentals; supplemental light; a dance floor; and auxiliary insurance to protect the cars. It may still be fairly inexpensive, but crunch some numbers and discuss it with your friend's father. Compare the costs to the costs of a hotel rental and determine which is more cost effective. You may be willing to pay a little extra for such a unique location.

Accessorizing Your Wedding Within Your Budget

You'd be surprised at the innovative and inexpensive ways you can accessorize your wedding. From programs to flowers to favors, the savings can add up! With a little advanced planning and some creative thinking, you can shave hundreds to thousands of dollars off your budget while maintaining a beautiful ambiance.

Make Your Own Wedding Program

Don't bother hiring someone to design and print your program. If you can type on a computer, then you can do it yourself.

Scrimp & Save

Print copies of your own homemade programs from your computer, or copy them at your local printer.

Programs can be as simple as a sheet of pretty paper (placed on each guest's seat) listing the members of the wedding party, those who are doing readings, and short descriptions of other elements relating to the ceremony.

•

Consider using your programs as nice souvenirs instead of buying favors.

Scrimp & Save

To save money, place one program on every other chair at the ceremony, or have ushers distribute one per single, couple, or family at the entrance.

Budget Tips for Hiring a Florist

Shop around. Price ranges and packages will vary greatly, and you may be pleasantly surprised to find that smaller vendors are more flexible with their prices.

•

Read the fine print of the contracts, and ask lots of questions. As experts, florists can often suggest cost savings or small touches that you may not have considered.

I had a friend who was trying to break into the floral business do my flowers. We had the largest, most beautiful centerpieces that were made of exotic flowers on pedestals sitting on mirrors with votive candles around them. The flowers in the huppah were also extraordinary. We had forty dining tables, a cake table, head table, guest book table, plus all the bouquets (eight attendants each plus moms, etc.) and huppah, and greenery at the ends of the aisles all for under $2,000.

—*Barbara B., Irvine, CA*

- -

Look at photo albums of the florists' work in addition to some of their live arrangements.

•

Come prepared with floral images that you have collected from magazines and Web sites.

•

Bring a color swatch from your dress and bridesmaid dresses so the florist can offer you economical tips to complement your color scheme.

•

When you have narrowed your choice to a few florists, have them give you the dates of their current scheduled events and locations where you can take a peek at their live work.

•

Ask for reference letters or thank-you notes the florist has received from previous clients.

•

Call their references (usually bride's or mother's of the brides) to get personal feedback.

Scrimp & Save

If you have total confidence in your florist's taste and abilities and you want to save the most, allow him or her to select the freshest and cheapest flowers available the week of your wedding and make your arrangements from those that are least expensive.

To eliminate delivery fees, impose on a friend to transport your flowers.

Super Duper Deal

Consider finding a floral-school student or new florist who is breaking into the field who is seeking experience. You'll get better prices.

Give florists your budget up front, and be sure they can work within it.

Bridal and Attendants' Bouquets

Hand-tied bouquets are becoming popular for the wedding party. Good news: They cost less than the traditional plastic florist bouquet holders and look as though they were freshly picked for the ceremony!

•

Instead of elaborate ribbons, tulle, and flower bundles, consider having the bridesmaid's bouquets be fresh-cut flowers tied with a simple satin ribbon.

Scrimp & Save

Consider carrying one simple, large flower such as a calla lily tied in a beautiful ribbon as the bouquet or three large sunflowers, or use this idea for the bridesmaids' flowers. It is classy and cost-effective.

One bride had an usher give a single flower to each guest sitting closest to the aisle before the ceremony began. As the bride walked down the aisle, she literally collected her bouquet from her guests. The maid of honor quickly bundled and tied all the flowers together for her.

●

Mix fresh and preserved flowers in the bouquets to save on costs.

Scrimp & Save

If you are carrying silk or dried flowers, be sure to have a sachet of potpourri attached to the handle of the bouquet, or use a scented spray to enhance the bouquet's aroma. This costs almost nothing, but adds a nice touch.

Follow an ancient custom: Include ivy in the bridal bouquet, which is inexpensive and can later be planted in your garden as a living reminder of the wedding celebration.

•

Eliminate bouquets for grandmothers and mothers of the bride and groom. Instead, opt for a single stem for them to carry.

Be Your Own Florist: Budget and Concerns

If you do your own flowers, beware that it is more time-consuming and time-sensitive than you might realize. Do you really want to be stressing over flower quality, quantities, or refrigeration the few final days before your wedding?

•

If you do decide to do them yourself, for budget and time considerations, your best bet may be potted plants, bowls with a few floating votives and flowers, or silk arrangements.

•

Order fresh-cut flowers through your local grocer or home-goods wholesale supplier. You may be pleasantly surprised by their prices and quality. (Or, order premade centerpieces and bouquets directly through them.)

I made my own table-number plaques at a paint-your-own ceramics studio. I used two-by-two-inch ceramic tiles and on the front painted the table number (using different designs on each one: hearts, plaids, etc.). On the back, I printed our names and wedding date. I had the ceramics store drill two holes at the top of each tile, and then strung organza ribbon through them and hung them from the centerpieces. They were a huge hit, and it was special to have done them myself.

—*Kelly B., Washington, D.C.*

Potted topiaries—climbing ivy designed around mesh frames in specific shapes—are a fun alternative to floral centerpieces. Add some ribbon or a few attached flower blooms to spiff them up.

I did my own flowers with small, green, ivy topiaries that I decorated with white twinkling lights and gardenias. I planted them in generic, terra-cotta garden pots that were 99 cents each, and I spray-painted them gold. The centerpieces served as a door prize for the guest at the table who had a penny (which the caterer had placed) under their saucer. I enjoyed the process so much, and people raved about my creations, so I actually broke into the flower business after my wedding and pursued a new career as a florist!

—*Jennifer R., West Palm Beach, FL*

Flowers and candles floating in a fishbowl or clear glass vase are also simple, inexpensive, yet pretty ways to decorate your table.

•

One bride who had an "island/nautical" theme wedding used live goldfish as her centerpieces. A guest at each table took them home as a favor.

Scrimp & Save

Add a drop of food coloring to clear vases or bowls for a color-coordinated effect that complements your wedding scheme.

Consider using silk flowers. They can be prepared far in advance, and you don't have to worry about them wilting at the reception.

•

Look into renting ready-made floral centerpieces that can be used one time for a fraction of the cost of fresh flowers.

Frugal Freebie

When the ceremony is over, reuse the loose-cut bridesmaids' bouquets by putting them into prepared fresh-water vases to serve as the centerpieces for the reception and to decorate the cake and head tables.

If your wedding ceremony or reception occurs near a pond, pool, or fountain, use floating flowers and candles. The effect is dazzling and romantic, and the cost is minimal.

Flower-Buying Tips

1. Avoid orchids and roses—they are the most expensive flowers.

2. Avoid white flowers as they show brown edges easily and are harder for florists to work with (and therefore more costly).

3. Use less costly flowers and greenery as filler such as carnations, daisies, baby's breath, ivy, and fern.

4. Select flowers that are in season for your wedding.

5. Try to use flowers that are grown locally so you will save on the shipping costs built into flower pricing.

6. Consider using potted plants as centerpieces instead of fresh-cut flowers. Better yet, grow them yourself in advance of the wedding. Plus, they can be replanted in your (or your guests') garden later.

7. Moss serves as a great filler for holes in arrangements or to hide dirt at the base of pots and green foam centers.

8. If you live near any farms, see if they have fresh-grown flowers for sale. They can cost a fraction of the price of even the cheapest wholesalers.

9. Spray-paint branches to use as filler.

10. Ask friends who live near the site if they have gardens and would be willing to donate cuttings from them to be used for your wedding decor.

Alternatives to Flowers

Balloons are cheap, fun, colorful, and festive. They match any decor and can be arranged easily as centerpieces, around chairs, aisles, and more.

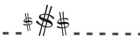

Scrimp & Save

Cost-effective alternatives to floral centerpieces include balloons and confetti; baskets of fresh fruit, gourds, and autumn leaves (if seasonal); pretty tissues, fabric squares, or gift wrap; flat circular mirrors with votives arranged on top; or a few framed pictures of the bride and groom in fun scenarios, arranged in a circle facing the guests.

Candles and votives should be used everywhere, from centerpieces to other parts of the reception area. They are much less costly than fresh flowers and create a romantic ambiance. Tea lights are cheap, too, and can burn for hours both indoors and out.

Frugal Freebie

Tall candelabras with their bases garnished in greenery or with vines and flowers climbing up the base offer a dramatic effect and save on the cost of flowers. Many sites already have candelabras or other floral containers that they use as centerpieces for events that you can use or borrow for your event free of charge.

Use one wide, tall candle (or grouping of various-sized candles) as your centerpiece and decorate the base with tulle fabric or ivy, or even sit them on a round mirror. Voilà! A simple, frugal centerpiece, with few frills and very little fuss!

•

Fresh fruit arranged in bowls or baskets, vegetables, cornucopias filled with seasonal leaves, branches, gourds, or other items pertaining to the region where you get married also work as centerpieces for a fraction of the cost of fresh flowers.

I got this idea from a New York City window display and modeled my homemade centerpieces after them. I bought thirteen tall, wide glass vases found at a floral mart for $2.99 a piece and filled them with water. Any clear container will do, though. In three jars I placed a dozen lemons, three more with oranges, three with apples, three with limes and the head table had a larger jar with a mixture of the eye-pleasing, colorful, whimsical, inexpensive fruits. These served as my unique, summertime centerpieces for a brunch wedding. At each table, a lucky guest went home with the centerpiece as a wedding favor.

—*Rachel S., New York, NY*

Tiny vases with individual flowers in them serve as an inexpensive centerpiece when grouped together and also double as a nice favor for guests. You can find tiny glass or ceramic vases for under a dollar at wholesalers, flea markets, and even through your grocer.

Decorations on a Dime

The flowers that decorate the ceremony site can be transported to the reception.

•

Use the bridesmaid bouquets to adorn the cake-cutting table so it looks nicely decorated for photos.

•

Save on flower and greenery costs by getting married in a garden or other outdoor setting.

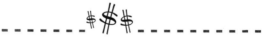

Scrimp & Save

Use greenery such as ivy, fern, and vines on church pews, huppahs, and trellises or large flower blooms to cover more surface area and get more bang for your buck.

- - - - - - - - - - - - - - - - - - -

Tulle, that scratchy crinoline fabric, can be purchased by the yard rather inexpensively at most fabric stores. It can be knotted, draped, or tied in bows around chairs, pots, a wedding canopy, and as aisle or pew markers.

•

Rose petals, confetti, glitter, or shaved chocolate all work as inexpensive table accents to scatter around the base of your centerpiece.

- - - - - - - - - - - - - - -

Frugal Freebie

Twinkling white lights can be borrowed from any friends who use them to decorate their homes during the holidays. If you plan to use these lights, begin to gather them in advance. They are virtually free and make for a beautiful effect!

- - - - - - - - - - - - - - - - - -

Dim the lights in the reception room to add romantic ambiance and set the mood. Dimmer lights may also mean less focus on your decor, food, and centerpieces so you can cut back a bit on these items.

●

Getting married around a holiday may solve your decorating worries. Many halls are already covered in flowers, decorations, and other festive accents to acknowledge the particular holiday.

●

Find out if another wedding is occurring around the same time as yours, and contact that bride to see if there are any decorations, flowers, or other rental costs you can share.

I had a Disney theme wedding and used Disneyland snow globes as my centerpieces surrounded by Disney characters and small flower vases. For table assignment cards, I used Disney photo magnet frames with each guest's name and table number inserted. Guests later took these magnets home as favors. The cost was much less than flower arrangements and printed table cards.

—*Kim F., Fort Lauderdale, FL*

Low-Cost (or No-Cost!) Favors

Inexpensive homemade wedding favors include painted napkin rings with your names and wedding date; cookies, fudge, or chocolates wrapped in tissue or clear cellophane with ribbon; or tiny potted plants.

●

Instead of the typical Jordan almonds wrapped in tulle, some couples give guests a packet of flower seeds with their names and wedding date attached; guests can plant the seeds at their homes in honor of the wedding.

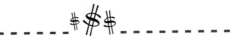

Scrimp & Save

Make your own wedding favors. Arts and crafts stores have many inexpensive trinkets, beads, lace, sequins, and pearls. They even carry small figurines that can be painted to go atop your wedding cake or in centerpieces. If you have creative friends or family members, enlist their help!

Purchase boxes of tiny undecorated bottles of bubbles; then add your own ribbon around the neck of the bottle. They serve as great favors, and guests can blow them during the ceremony or as you exit instead of throwing rice or flower petals.

•

Golf tees, pens, pencils, or key chains with your name and wedding date printed on them can be ordered in bulk from many mail-order companies, catalogs, or Internet sites for a very low price.

Super Duper Deal

Buy miniature chocolate bars in bulk and remove the outer printed wrapper on each. Then tie a ribbon that corresponds to your wedding colors around the foil inner wrapper and put one at each place. Or, make your own personalized labels on your computer with a message to your guests, meaningful quote, poem, or scanned photo.

Make your own chocolates or lollipops using molds purchased at a crafts store. Hearts, flowers, doves, or other romantic shapes can be tied up with pretty ribbon or wrapped in cellophane bags.

•

Purchase adhesive magnets, peel back the adhesive paper, and attach any photo, computerized message, or image for personalized reminders of your event.

Scrimp & Save

Use tiny tea light votive holders, costing under $1 apiece, on your tables, and send them home with your guests as favors.

Other inexpensive favors include plastic picture frames; fancy coffee beans or tea leaves in a bag or mug; bath soaps; a special message, quote, or poem rolled up in a homemade scroll tied with ribbon; or a cassette tape or CD with your favorite songs in a personalized box.

•

Make a contribution to a charity of your choice, and announce to guests that in lieu of favors, you and your groom have made a donation in honor of your wedding day and guests.

•

For do-it-yourself souvenir matchbooks, purchase plain white matchbooks in bulk and add a computer-made adhesive label with your names and wedding date. Or, scan a photo of the two of you onto labels to adhere to the matchbooks.

•

Put a sticker or special marking underneath one chair or coffee saucer at each table, and announce that the person in that seat may take home the centerpiece arrangement as a favor.

•

The cheapest favor of all: Eliminate favors altogether!

We did not give favors to everyone. This is a tradition that people can cut back on unless the favors are really wonderful, in my opinion. We did cut compact discs, though. My husband loves music, and his friend had a burner. We printed our own liner notes from a computer program and a cover that corresponded with our wedding program cover. We gave the CDs only to good friends and family. We still get comments about the mix, and people wonder when we are cutting our next album—probably for our first anniversary!

—*Sarah S., Algona, IA*

Q. *My friend is suggesting I use silk and plastic flowers to save money. Is that too tacky?*

A. Using artificial flowers instead of fresh flowers is not tacky, as long as the flowers you choose are attractive—many times people can't even tell the difference. The bright side to that is you'll be able to easily preserve them . . . forever.

Another option is to go to the grocery store or buy your flowers wholesale. Or, you can skip flowers altogether and use balloon bouquets, fruit bowls, or other less expensive arrangements. If you go with something you can re-use, you have a constant reminder of your special day.

9

Dressing the Bride and Groom on a Budget

The bridal gown does not need to cost as much as a small car, especially for an outfit you'll probably only wear once! Ditto for the groom's ensemble. So how can you two be a vision without spending your entire bank account? There are lots of tricks of the trade that can clue you in to some frugal fashioning.

Preparing for the Purchase

Have an idea of what you are looking for in your dress, so you have narrowed down some possibilities before heading to the stores. Doing some homework in advance may make things easier and less time-consuming, as well as keep you on track and within budget.

•

Many Web sites have huge databases with thousands of gowns cross-referenced by style, price, and designer (see pertaining section on page 191 for a listing).

•

Consult wedding magazines, photographers' wedding albums, and bridal salons for low-cost ideas.

•

Bring photos, clippings, and any other ideas to see if the salon, retailer, or dressmaker can inexpensively replicate your visions.

•

Price shop and compare.

Go to a small town near you and have the dress made. My skirt only cost $40 because it was simple and straight, and you didn't need to be Vera Wang to make it!

—*Sarah S., Algona, IA*

Wedding Retailer Budget Tips

Be up-front about your budget, and don't have the salesperson bring you dresses that are beyond your price range. Out of sight, out of mind!

●

If you purchase your gown from a retailer, order it at least six months prior to your wedding date to allow for errors in size, style, or shipping. Your don't want to get stuck paying extra rush fees.

●

Alterations can be time-consuming and during peak wedding seasons difficult to schedule. Be sure you understand the policies and alteration schedule of your gown maker or distributor before committing to buying your dress there. Find out if there are fees for alterations.

•

Read all of the fine print in your dress contract—especially regarding your deposit, arrival dates, alteration policies, and damages the dress may have. Get everything in writing.

•

Inquire about return policies or deposit refunds in case your wedding is delayed or altogether canceled. You never know, and it is best to be prepared.

Super Duper Deal

Try on bridesmaid dresses and if you find one that you like, see if it comes in white. Order it for your wedding dress for a fraction of the cost of a "real" wedding gown.

Be careful about what size gown the bridal store orders for you. Unless alteration fees are included, order a dress that most closely resembles your current size.

•

Avoid shopping in wedding salons on the weekends as the salespeople will be busy and you may get frustrated in a hectic salon.

•

Be flexible with your preferences. You may be pleasantly surprised to end up with a dress that was not what you had originally envisioned.

•

Keep a copy of your measurements—those taken at the wedding store—to ensure that the staff is ordering the appropriate size.

•

Don't get measured after a large meal or when you are bloated.

Discounts on Dresses

Buy a gown off the rack at a department store in the eveningwear or sale sections after the holiday season or in the prom section after prom season.

As far as frugal weddings go, I'm sure I come close to winning the prize for least expensive gown: $99 at Jessica McClintock in San Francisco. Can you top that?

—*Debbie D., Newport Beach, CA*

Yes, but just barely . . .

My wedding dress cost only $65, which was quite cheap even by 1983 standards! I purchased it off the rack. It was considered a "summer informal." It was very pretty and traditional in design. And, although it did not have a long flowing train, it did have a bustle. My mother was actually quite worried when she heard what I had paid, but it worked out just fine. Having just celebrated eighteen years of marriage, I guess everything else did as well.

—*Beth S., Irvine, CA*

Shop at used clothing stores, sample sales, and trunk shows for bridal gowns. The Bridal Garden for instance is a shop in New York where designers donate runway dresses at great prices.

•

Go for a simple dress without a lot of beading, lacework, and layered fabrics. The more intricate the dress, usually the more expensive it is.

Super Duper Deal

Check local newspapers or wedding Web site message boards for wedding dresses for sale. You may find one in your size that has never been worn or worn just once for a fraction of the cost you were considering.

Consignment stores, discount warehouses, outlet stores, and renting are all less expensive options to buying a full-priced dress.

•

Buy a simple, flattering white dress from a department store or boutique. Use this as the basis for a gown that you or a seamstress can detail with lace, beading, and other finery. You'll spend a fraction of the cost and will have a totally unique dress!

•

Brides also redesign and alter their mother's, sister's, or close friend's gowns. Remember that a dress can be worn more than once.

My mother and I have the same body shape. I wore her beautiful dress almost twenty-five years after she did. It needed very little altering and had sentimental meaning to me since it was hers.

—*Linda R., Houston, TX*

Frugal Freebie

Borrow, borrow, borrow—veils, dresses, shoes, wedding-day jewelry, and other accessories. Friends and relatives are usually more than willing to see their items used and appreciated again by another bride.

Design your own gown with special touches that accentuate your body type. Surprisingly, custom gowns can sometimes be more cost-effective than those bought off the rack.

Frugal Freebie

If you have a friend who can sew or, better yet, if you know a seamstress or tailor personally, ask if he or she will make you a dress as your wedding gift. Offer to purchase the fabric and pattern, and thank them for their time to fit and make your dress.

If you are gutsy, hire a student at a local fashion institute to take on designing your wedding dress as a project to add to his or her portfolio.

More Frugal Fashion Tips

Many brides are tired of the idea of wearing their dress only once, so they buy a dress that can later be shortened, altered, or even dyed a different color to get more use out of it.

•

Don't change into a going-away outfit or even purchase a special one. Rather, exit as you entered: as the glowing bride.

•

Check at dry cleaners to see if any brides have not picked up their dresses. Many times the costs are too much for cleaning or preserving, and some brides end up leaving their dresses. If you pay the cleaning bill, they may be willing to give you an almost-new unclaimed gown.

•

Purchase the dress that is the sample size if it fits you or just needs minor alterations. You'll probably have to pay to have the dress cleaned because many have tried it on, but you may wind up saving hundreds or even thousands of dollars.

- - - - - - - - - - - - - - - - - -

Frugal Freebie

Borrow other wedding items—for example, a garter from a friend who has been married and yarmulkes from your local temple.

- -

Purchase last year's model just as you would a car. Gowns that have been discontinued or need to be moved out of stock to make room for the new designs cost less. Ask retailers when they have these sales or bring in their new gowns.

Cheap Feet

Any white pump that is not labeled a "wedding" shoe will cost significantly less than a salon bridal shoe.

Scrimp & Save

Buy a white- or cream-colored shoe that you'll wear again. One bride wore wedding boots with buttons up the sides, which she later dyed black to wear in the winter months.

For extra comfort and practicality, some brides today wear pearl, sequin, and lace-decorated white sneakers to the wedding. If you choose to do so, you may want to still have a pair of dressier shoes for your photos, first dance, and other times when your feet may be more visible.

•

Decorate your own tennis shoes with sequins, lace, and beading.

•

All-white tennis shoes from a shoe outlet or simple ballet or bedroom slippers double as comfortable, inexpensive bridal footwear.

•

Another gutsy bride wore clogs and later went barefoot to stay comfortable on the dance floor. The groom, in turn, wore black suede tennis shoes with his tuxedo.

•

Buy inexpensive, comfortable pantyhose. Avoid beaded, lace, or fancy garter-clipped ones. Have an extra pair on standby in case of runs.

Budget Hair and Makeup

Do your own, or have a friend do your hair and makeup.

•

Go to a department store makeup counter and have a few of the consultants make you up on various days. If

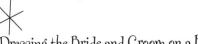
you find someone you like, offer him or her a job moonlighting for your wedding.

Frugal Freebie

If possible, go to the department store the morning of your wedding or before photos to have your makeup done at the counter for free. Many beauticians would be thrilled to make up a bride. (Try a few out in advance of your wedding date so you can know whose products, colors, etc., you like.)

Skip the veil and opt for a borrowed pearl barrette, comb, or fresh flower buds from your florist.

Try on a variety of veils at your dress fittings. Then go to a fabric store that carries wedding tulle. The staff there can advise you on how much to purchase, and they have accessories like combs, hair bands, and tiaras in addition to decorations. Instead of paying more than $100 to $200 for your veil, you can easily have one made or make your own for $10 to $30. And, while you're at it, have a white Bible cover (if you plan to carry a Bible)

made with matching decorations and make and a ring bearer's pillow.

—*Charlene W., Lakeland, FL*

- -

Budget Groom's Attire

For ease and comfort, wear your own black dress shoes instead of renting.

•

Buying a tuxedo may wind up being more cost-effective if you plan to attend additional black-tie events in the future.

•

Wear a dark suit with a tie (or bow tie) instead of a tuxedo.

•

Borrow a tux from a friend who is your size but not in the wedding party.

•

Borrow studs and cufflinks from a father, cousin, or other friend or relative.

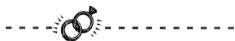

Q. *My friend has offered to loan me a gown. It fits perfectly and is exactly what I want, but she's no longer married. Is it true that it's bad luck to borrow her gown?*

A. Definitely not! Your wedding is your own unique, special day. Unless you are truly superstitious, borrow the gown and put the money you save toward another element of your wedding that is really important to you.

10

Frugally Hiring the Help

You want to have a strong group of professionals working on your wedding, but at the same time you don't want to blow your budget. Old-timers with years of experience don't necessarily translate to the best there is. You may be surprised to find people just starting out in the wedding business who are less expensive, harder working, and guaranteed dependable. Hiring your wedding support network requires patience, research, and determination if you want to be frugal and savvy.

The Officiant

A religious leader or judge who is also a close friend often will refuse to charge a fee for conducting your ceremony. Be sure to get him or her a personal gift, write a special thank-you note, and perhaps consider donating to the house of worship or other meaningful charity in the person's name in lieu of monetary compensation. (It will still cost you less than paying standard fees!)

•

Look into officiants' backgrounds, references, or credentials to be sure they are authorized to perform marriages in your state and that their fees are competitive.

•

Instead of having a priest, rabbi, or judge as your officiant, have a close friend marry you: perhaps the person who introduced the two of you, a significant family friend, or even a member of your wedding party. Ask a wedding coordinator, do research on the Internet, or check with your justice of the peace about requirements for becoming a wedding officiant in your state. In most states, a person can obtain an inexpensive certificate that allows him or her to legally preside over your ceremony.

The Photographer

Hire a professional photographer for the ceremony and reception, but also see if a close friend, relative, or a photography student would be willing to take candid pictures with his or her own camera. Some of their pictures will come out even better than the professional's, at a fraction of the cost.

●

Skip ordering the photographer's albums or frames. Instead, register for these or make them yourself.

●

If your photographer's company also handles videography, you may get a price break by going with just one vendor. Also, find out if you get a discount if you order your video and photos at the same time.

Scrimp & Save

Use disposable cameras on the reception tables for friends and family to take candid or more casual shots. Having them all developed simultaneously may get you a discount.

Look into hiring a photographer from a local newspaper as opposed to a "wedding" photographer. He or she may be willing to moonlight and do the job for you at a fraction of the cost. Just be sure to have lists ready for this person of what groupings you would like, your expectations of his or her role during the ceremony and reception, and other details that are important to you.

●

If your photographer does not charge an hourly fee, request that he or she arrive before the wedding to get photos of your guests arriving as well as behind-the-scenes pictures of you getting ready.

●

Have only color photos taken at your wedding. Black-and-whites are usually more expensive to process. Plus, color photos can be reprinted in black and white if you so desire. Black-and-white film, however, cannot be converted to color; it can only be hand-tinted.

●

Consider having digital photos taken by a friend or photographer. They can be downloaded and printed immediately. Many photographers can have complete digital photo albums ready for guests to see by the end of the reception.

●

See if you can pay the photographer for his or her time but process the film yourself.

•

Ask about keeping or buying the negatives of your event.

•

Purchase a simple album with basic shots of the wedding. You can always add more to it later when your budget allows.

Questions and Negotiating Tactics for Hiring a Photographer

1. Will you include the proofs in the cost of your photo package? (These pictures are great to send with thank-you notes or to make up minialbums for grandmothers or special relatives. Also, having the proofs will eliminate the need to order extra individual photos for some family members who request them. You can give them a framed proof instead.)
2. Will you bring two working cameras to our wedding, just in case one of them malfunctions or the film is bad?
3. Will you follow a detailed list of all the formal shots we need taken, specifying the particular groupings we would like?
4. What are your costs for hourly fees versus package deals?
5. How long do you keep our negatives in case we want to purchase some more photos at a later date?
6. Is there an additional fee if you bring an assistant?

7. Do you take any breaks or require a meal?

8. How do you charge for overtime?

9. What type of insurance coverage do you carry for lost or damaged photos?

10. May I look at a book of unedited proofs from a recent wedding of comparable budget that you have shot? (It will give you a general idea of what to expect and how many photos come out as rejects.)

11. How do you handle photo touch-ups such as red eye, overexposure, or glare?

12. Are you a member in good standing with any professional associations?

We chose photographers who were just starting out in the business and wanted to build a portfolio. We were skittish about it at first, but they were incredible—a husband-and-wife team. They worked very hard because it was only their second wedding, but they charged significantly less and even gave us all the negatives and the proof book for free!

—*Barbara B., Irvine, CA*

Hiring the Videographer

Get everything in writing, and read all of the fine print in your contracts. Be sure you understand all of the points of your contract, including issues of deposit refunds and loss or damage to pictures, before signing on any dotted lines.

•

View current samples of the person's work.

•

Check the videographer's references.

•

Reach an agreement about how many guest interviews you want included in your tape. If the videographer will not be bringing an assistant, you don't want him or her tied up interviewing guests while other events are happening that should be recorded.

•

Ask to review the raw footage of your video prior to the final edits so that you can choose to eliminate any elements that you don't feel compelled to include, such as extralong toasts or too much footage of the dance floor.

•

See if the videographer will tape your ceremony and just an abbreviated version of your reception. Eliminate personal toasts and extraneous details so you can cut back on costs.

Super Duper Deal

Have your videographer tape the entire event, but purchase it unedited and do it yourself.

Do not request any special effects or music that may cost you extra.

●

Put your videographer and photographer in contact before the wedding so they can make sure that their supplemental lighting and equipment will not conflict with each other's work.

Budget Alternatives to a Professional Videographer

If you have little or no budget to videotape your wedding, try calling the audiovisual department at a local high school or community college and hire a student to tape it. These student-produced videos can have loads of fun effects, music, and audio and often come out as well as a professional video.

- - - - - - - - - -  - - - - - - - - - -

I had no plans or budget for a video of my wedding until my friend suggested I try the local high school to see if I could get a student from their video department to do it for me inexpensively. I hired a high school senior who wore a suit, taped my entire wedding ceremony and reception, and only charged me $100 plus a wedding meal to keep him energized. He did an amazing job with lots of special effects!

—*Melissa D., Boca Raton, FL*

- -

If you really don't care about a professional-looking video, get a tripod and place your video camera on it. Point it at the alter area where you and your groom will stand. Have a friend push the record button at the right time and see what you get. At minimum, you'll have the audio of your ceremony with some video footage to boot!

•

Hire a camera operator from a local news station who may want to moonlight at your ceremony.

Frugal Freebie

Ask friends and family who have video cameras to tape your wedding ceremony and reception. Then combine the best segments from each, and you'll have your own tape for free!

Hiring the Musicians

Deejays are typically a less expensive option than a live band. Decide with your fiancé how important this element of your wedding is to you and what your budget limitations are.

Scrimp & Save

Hire a brand-new deejay who is looking to add to his or her experience and will give you a bargain price in exchange for some exposure.

Don't rely solely on demo videotapes or audio music. Check out your prospective deejay or band at a live event prior to hiring them or, at minimum, prior to your wedding so that you can express your own desires and expectations.

•

Check references on your band or deejay from multiple sources: brides and grooms who have used them, wedding coordinators or hotels that have worked with them, and so on.

Have a band with fewer musicians. Instead of having a ten-piece band, we had five and it was still perfect. Also, have one videographer instead of two. We found out about this idea a bit too late to benefit, but hire the videographer and photographer from the same company, and you'll usually save some money as opposed to using two different companies.

—*Yanina F., Irvine, CA*

Read the deejay's or band's contract closely with regard to their policy on overtime payments as well as any hidden costs you may incur such as setup and take-down fees, permit fees, meal costs, frequency of breaks, or insurance.

●

You and the groom are the stars of the evening, not the musical performers. Make your wishes clear up-front.

●

Choose your song list in advance of the wedding to ensure that you and your guests enjoy the selections.

●

Skip the costly extras that deejays or bands may provide such as maracas, costume paraphernalia, bubble and smoke machines, fancy lighting, and even backup dancers to mingle with the guests on the dance floor. These added elements are not worth the extra expense.

Questions to Ask
When Hiring a Band

1. What music selections will be played during your breaks? (There is nothing worse than eating dinner to rock 'n' roll if you would prefer soft jazz.)
2. How many breaks do you take?
3. What will you wear?

4. When do you next play an event so we can see you perform live?
5. Can we have references to call?
6. Will you follow our song list provided in advance of the wedding to ensure that we and our guests enjoy the selection?

7. Can you accommodate special requests at the event, or do you only play from your preselected song list?
8. Will you learn to play songs that we want that are not on your permanent list?
9. Are you members of a musicians' union or other professional association?

Ceremony Music Bargains and Do-It-Yourself Music

Instead of using a string quartet or organist during the processional, consider using a friend who plays guitar or sings for a very personal and cost-effective alternative.

Our friend is a guitar player at a local café. We asked him to sing our favorite song during the ceremony. It was a great and cost-effective personal touch!

—*Kim M., Minneapolis, MN*

See if the band or deejay that plays at your reception can send someone from their group early to cover the ceremony music. It will cost you less than hiring a separate professional.

Consider using prerecorded music during the ceremony.

Frugal Freebie

Some computer-literate couples are using an MP3 player at their weddings that organizes preselected songs via your computer and plays them at the reception or during the dance portion of your celebration.

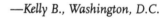

We made our own CDs for music during the rehearsal dinner and reception dinner. We even included the wedding songs of all of our friends in attendance on the CDs, too!

—*Kelly B., Washington, D.C.*

Bride and Groom Transportation

Consider alternatives to the traditional (and expensive) limousine exit. Tap into personal contacts and resources for anyone who has access to a horse-drawn carriage, boat, hot-air balloon, taxi, streetcar, old-fashioned car, motorcycle, convertible, or even a tandem bicycle if your dress permits. Choose a fun and clever send-off that suits your style, budget, and wedding theme.

My grandfather's friend has an antique car collection. He provided us with a free, glamorous Rolls-Royce to use as our exit vehicle!

—*Joyce Z., Cherry Creek, CO*

Super Duper Deal

If you use a limousine, see if you can pay by the hour or à la carte. In other words, hire the car for the hour to drive you to the site and the hour to whisk you away. You might be able to avoid paying for the extra waiting time in between.

- -

Arrange for food and beverage to be waiting for you in your transportation vehicle in case you are thirsty or hungry. Don't let the limousine staff provide any alcohol, though—they generally charge you more for it.

Super Duper Deal

Hire a town car or a fun convertible instead of a limousine to drive you and your spouse off after the ceremony.

- -

Frugal Freebie

Eliminate the send-off cost altogether, and simply leave the wedding and head straight down the hotel hall to the honeymoon suite.

- -

Q. *Should we bother to go to the expense of dance lessons for our first dance, or can we skip that to save?*

A. When all eyes are on you, it is a nice touch to look like you know what you are doing as opposed to rocking back and forth for your first dance. Do what I did: Instead of signing up for expensive Arthur Murray dance lessons, check with your local college or community center's dance program. We contacted the ballroom dance instructor of our local university ballroom dance club and asked if he would moonlight and offer us a few private dance lessons to help choreograph our first dance. We brought a tape of our song, had a blast, and paid only $50 for three private half-hour lessons. Or, at least have someone teach you a few dance moves that you two can repeat and feel comfortable doing together. You will probably find these private lessons to be cheaper than formal, group dance classes.

11

Economical Ideas to Eat, Drink, and Get Married

Moments after you hear, "I now pronounce you man and wife," it's time to eat the all-important food! What wedding would be complete without delighting the guests' palettes? Check out these frugal options to scrimp and save.

Hiring the Caterer

For hotel or banquet hall receptions, set up a meeting with the caterer and map out your budgetary constraints, dietary restrictions, dream menu, and other food-related desires.

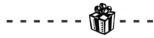

Frugal Freebie

Most caterers will offer you tastings of menu items so that you can sample the various foods that could be served at your event. Take advantage of the free tastings and bring your fiancé along!

Determine whether a sit-down meal, a buffet, or a hearty hors d'oeuvres and cake reception is more cost-effective—the options run the gamut.

•

Don't accept the first number that a caterer throws out. Negotiate until you are comfortable with the price.

•

Be sure to ask your caterer what is the latest possible date you can submit your head count for guests. Many guests RSVP at the last minute, and you do not want to be penalized or pay for extra meals that go uneaten.

•

Ask for a simple, inexpensive plate of food (perhaps a pared-down version of your wedding meal) for your band, deejay, wedding coordinator, photographer, videographer, and so on, if their contracts so specify.

Questions for the Caterer

1. May we call on your references?
2. Can we set up a tasting of some sample dishes that fit into our budget?
3. Are you insured and licensed to protect against any unforeseen problems?
4. What china will the food will be served on? (Be sure that it doesn't clash with your centerpieces, table covers, or food presentation.)
5. Can you get us any price breaks on beverages or our wedding cake?
6. Will you offer a less expensive children's menu if we invite youngsters to our wedding?

Cheap Eats

Some receptions provide personalized menus on the tables with the couple's names and wedding date followed by a listing of the courses and how they are prepared. If you include this touch, make the menus on your computer instead of paying the site or caterer to do so.

•

Stick to chicken or pasta dishes as opposed to beef, lamb, or fish, which tend to be more expensive entrées.

- - - - - - - - - - - - - - - - - - - -

Super Duper Deal

Visit a local culinary institute or cooking school to see if any students or chefs there would be interested in catering your reception. The students may charge a great deal less, need the experience, and will probably work even harder if they receive any class credit.

- - - - - - - - - - - - - - - - - - - -

If you have a set menu, consider eliminating the dessert course and having the wedding cake be offered alone as the dessert. Most people don't eat two desserts, anyway.

•

Select a menu of foods that are simple to prepare and not too labor-intensive for your catering staff.

•

A variety of foods presented in buffet-style food stations can be more cost-effective than a fixed menu since they do not require servers. Your guests also get to choose exactly the meal they want and enjoy it hot.

Scrimp & Save

One bride hired a local Girl Scout troop leader and six Girl Scouts to assist with serving and cleaning up at her reception. Since it was an hors d'oeuvres and light-fare event, their work mainly consisted of making sure platters were filled or replaced and keeping paper goods and supplies on the tables. The Girl Scouts got badges for donating their time, and the bride made a donation to the troop (which cost her much less than hiring a professional catering staff to do the same work).

Find out whether the cost of renting china is included in the price or additional.

•

Keep an accurate total of your costs so you are not surprised with unexpected bills after the event.

•

Have a brunch wedding, at which guests select from a make-your-own-omelet or Belgian waffle station, fruit platters, and a variety of pastries.

•

Hot tea with small pastries and finger sandwiches is another easy idea for brunch weddings.

•

Have a heavy beverage and hors d'oeuvres reception as opposed to a full sit-down meal.

•

Instead of paying servers, order vegetable and fruit platters, cheese and cracker trays, and other hors d'oeuvres that guests can serve themselves.

Super Duper Deal

If you are having a children's table, French fries, grilled cheese sandwiches, hamburgers, and macaroni and cheese are great, inexpensive choices for kiddy foods.

Frugal Freebie

Have a potluck wedding where guests bring a pre-assigned dish for all to share. (This option usually works better for smaller or second weddings.)

Having your reception at a restaurant may cut down significantly on catering and beverage costs since everything is prepared and servers are employed in-house.

Bargain Beverages

Serve only wine and beer at the wedding, and offer a cash bar for those who prefer other alcoholic beverages.

Frugal Freebie

Consider skipping the cocktail hour altogether, thus saving on the alcohol and hors d'oeuvres.

Remind servers only to offer refills on wine when the guest's glass is empty, not just half full.

We only had an open bar during the cocktail hour. Then, during dinner, only wine was served. An open bar for the entire event costs a fortune and isn't necessary. Also, we had a lunchtime wedding instead of an evening dinner wedding and saved on that, too.

—*Barbara B., Irvine, CA*

- - - - - - - - - - - - - - - - - -

Find out whether your establishment charges per bottle or per drink to guesstimate what your beverage costs will be.

- - - - - - - - - - - - - - - - - -

Super Duper Deal

If you bring in your own wine and liquor as opposed to using the reception hall's supplier, you may be charged a corkage fee per bottle, but this still might be more cost-effective. Plus, you may even be able to return unopened bottles to the place of purchase for a refund after your wedding.

- - - - - - - - - - - - - - - - - -

Be sure you will not be charged per head for alcoholic beverages for guests who are under legal drinking age. Have an accurate count of minors to provide to the caterer or beverage manager.

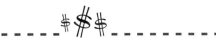

Scrimp & Save

Many universities offer bartending courses for students looking to make money on the side, and students may be less expensive than the on-site staff. If you choose to go with a student, make sure he or she will be insured, and also find out if bar supplies are available through the school or a subcontracted catering company to avoid having to rent or pay for these, too.

Scrimp & Save

Have water pitchers and wine bottles placed on the tables so guests can help themselves.

If you do a champagne toast, instruct the servers to fill glasses only halfway.

•

Use the table wine for toasts instead of purchasing champagne.

•

Cut out liquor and offer only nonalcoholic beverages and punch if you think your crowd wouldn't mind.

Let Them Eat Cake, but Not Too Much!

Bring your baker magazine clippings, photos, and clear descriptions of what you envision your cake to look like. Be certain that your reception hall approves of the baker or other outside food contractors that you are using, to avoid any insurance problems.

Scrimp & Save

Consider ordering your cake from a local grocery store, food warehouse, or small bakery. You may find their cakes to be just as tasty as the fancier bakeries' but much less expensive.

If you know a talented chef or baker, see if that person will make your cake as a wedding gift.

•

Use a small, one- or two-tier wedding cake to cut and feed each other at the reception, and have the same flavored sheet cakes presliced in the back by the caterer and ready to serve.

Our wedding cake choice was a two-tier carrot cake and only fed sixty guests. So we also bought cheaper sheet cakes and had a dessert table loaded with carrot cake, chocolate cake, Italian ricotta cake, sugar cookies, candy, fresh fruit, and sugared pecans that I made. We found some ladies in the area who made cakes and cookies from scratch, so the desserts were excellent and reasonably priced. People grazed the whole evening. We also had a buffet meal. Even I went through the line! Buffet is an underused option.

—*Sarah S., New York, NY*

Cost-Saving Ideas for Your Reception

Save time as well as money by eliminating some of the less essential traditions such as the garter throw or bouquet toss, if those activities are not as important to you.

•

Have open seating without place cards or table assignments. This will save time, money, and headaches in planning.

•

If you prefer assigned tables, skip the cost of place cards and calligraphy. Have a board that lists table assignments located in a prominent place, such as next to the sign-in or gift table.

Q. *My caterer keeps pushing certain foods on us, telling my fiancé and me that if we just serve chicken as our main course, people will realize that we are going cheap. Is that true, and what should we do?*

A. Insist on the chicken if that is what your budget allows. Entire cookbooks are dedicated to the different ways to prepare chicken, so be sure that your caterer come up with something that fits your budget and still looks appealing and impressive.

Also, you may want to think about finding a new caterer. If you are disagreeing about the menu and think that this vendor cannot execute your vision, hundreds of competitors would love to handle your event. Always be sure you are comfortable with the wedding experts you have hired, and don't be afraid to let a few go along the way if they cannot meet your expectations.

12

Other Frugal Ways to Wed

You now know about less costly alternatives to traditional weddings such as the destination wedding, but what are other economical ways to wed? Eloping and civil ceremonies are always a possibility. This chapter also covers the inexpensive declaration of love for those already married: a vow renewal or reaffirmation ceremony. Finally, how can you make your second weddings less costly than the first? Read on. . . .

Eloping and Civil Ceremonies

If you two feel that this is for you, go for it: Visit Vegas, or head to your justice of the peace or courthouse.

•

Eloping may severely reduce the number of gifts you receive. Some people may feel slighted that you did not include them in a ceremony or, at minimum, a reception.

•

On that note, consider having a reception, no matter how informal, to celebrate publicly and have your union recognized by family and friends. This allows those close to you to offer personal congratulations and feel included in your celebration.

After years of being engaged, we decided one morning to get married. We had talked about it for years and finally were determined to go for it. Instead of a big fanfare and going through all of the headaches involved in planning a wedding, we drove to our town hall and were married by a justice of the peace. We found our witnesses in the hallway on our way to sign papers! We had a casual but fun barbecue reception a few weeks later to celebrate our nuptials with family and friends. I highly recommend this route!

—*Kendra M., Tempe, AZ*

- -

Couples getting married for the second and third time often choose to elope for financial reasons.

•

Saying "I do" in a quick and simple civil ceremony is very old-fashioned, uniquely romantic, and certainly inexpensive.

•

If finances or timing are an issue, consider a civil ceremony and then a more elaborate celebration at a later date.

Lower-Cost Second Weddings

The biggest rule to remember is there are no rules. Just go with your instincts and be flexible when it comes to budget issues.

•

You can announce your news formally as you would for a first wedding, by contacting local papers, friends, and family and even sending out announcements, or you can be more low-key and budget-conscious, by simply calling those closest to you.

•

Announce your wedding plans at the same time you share your news. For example, if you plan to do a reception only and just include immediate family (or no one) at your ceremony, it may be good to be up-front with your plans when making your round of calls.

•

Many women who marry divorced or widowed men still want to have a big wedding with all the trimmings. Communicate your budget restrictions, and be open about feelings from the outset. In cases like this, the groom should indulge his bride.

•

When it is the man's first time and the woman's second, chances are you may be able to do something other than the large traditional wedding. Destination weddings, a smaller reception, or even eloping in Las Vegas may suit you just fine.

Frugal Benefits of Second Weddings

Remarrying is typically your chance to do anything and everything you wanted to do at your first but couldn't because of family issues or the pressure of tradition. So have fun and go for less costly approaches now, if that's your style.

•

Many second-time brides prefer to wear a cocktail dress or suit instead of an expensive wedding gown.

Frugal Freebie

Browse your closet as well as your family's and friend's for an appropriate ensemble for this special occasion.

You may be able to save friends and family the hassle and expense of gifts and registering since you probably already own many necessary or desired household items. If you do choose to register for gifts, smaller-ticket items would be appropriate.

•

In lieu of gifts, request that your guests make a donation to the charity of your choice.

Renewing Your Vows/ Reaffirmation Ceremonies

Renewing your vows can represent a new chapter in your lives. For example, if you have successfully left marriage counseling, you may want to renew your love for one another and symbolize a fresh start.

•

A vow renewal ceremony is the chance to have the wedding you never had. Maybe you eloped or did not have enough money for the wedding of your dreams. Renewing your vows later in your marriage can give you the wedding you always imagined (on a budget, of course!).

My husband and I wanted to have an excuse to meet up with good friends in Las Vegas, so we contacted them all via e-mail and invited them to join us in celebrating our vow renewal ceremony to commemorate our five-year wedding anniversary. In The Little White Chapel in Las Vegas, an Elvis impersonator remarried us and even serenaded us with "Love Me Tender." It was a blast, very inexpensive, and unforgettable.

—*Sandra, Portland, OR*

- -

You can even repropose with a ring, necklace, or other token of love, to symbolize your reunion. No jewelry or expense is required, however, and certainly the "two month's salary rule" need not apply!

•

Choose a special date for your event: Commemorate an anniversary, the day you first kissed, or even your engagement.

•

No hard-and-fast rules apply to a vow renewal ceremony. Feel free to be creative and budget-conscious.

•

Since you are already married, you can grab your partner and renew your vows, free of officiant fees and many other expenses!

•

Instead of traditional bridesmaids and groomsmen, ask important friends or relatives to walk in a processional, share the altar with you, or simply do readings or light a candle during your ceremony.

•

You should not feel obligated to give presents to your attendants. Just asking them to participate is enough of a gift.

Where to Renew Your Vows Inexpensively

You can renew almost anywhere—even at locations where it would be difficult to get married. No site fees need to be involved. Along the beach or on a public golf course is just as meaningful as at a fancy restaurant or hotel.

•

Return to your exact wedding location and re-create your wedding if your budget allows.

•

An exotic destination such as a romantic beach at sunset, barefoot on the sand, or atop a mountain on horseback will give your guests another reason to attend.

Frugal Freebie

Why not renew your vows at home? This location may truly be the most special place—after all, it's where you have built your life together!

Inexpensive Personal Touches

Create a home video or photo album of your years together, as well as your original wedding album, to share with your guests.

•

If you had a wedding video made, show clips of that to your guests.

•

Make a Web page and have it accessible by laptop at your gathering. You can also include still photos of you both scanned in for a slide show presentation via computer.

•

For free decorations, display photos from your wedding and other memorabilia (your wedding favors, wedding certificate, scrapbook, family photos, etc.).

Q. *My husband of ten years and I plan to renew our marriage vows. We're having a ceremony and reception but don't want guests to feel obligated to get us gifts. Many friends of ours have encouraged us to register, but we feel presumptuous in doing this in case it makes our guests feel that they have to spend on us. Any suggestions?*

A. The rules of reaffirmation ceremony etiquette have not really been written. If you really don't want any gifts from your guests, then write "No gifts, please," or "Your gift to us is your presence," on the invitation. If you think people want to get you something to celebrate your milestone, then by all means register for some items that you need. Perhaps you'd like to update some appliances or register for items you may not have selected for your wedding. There is nothing wrong with choosing what you want, but only share where you are registered if people ask. Expect to receive random gifts that you have not registered for, though, since many people will want to do their own thing and get you a token gesture.

13

Honeymoons on a Budget

The joy of being newlyweds on your honeymoon is a total high. Friends and family may urge you to splurge on an exceptional honeymoon, but you'll be surprised how many great deals are out there and tricks you can try to get some fantastic frugal alternatives.

Planning It Yourself on a Budget

Browse travel literature in bookstores and travel Web sites to shave hundreds of dollars off your trip by meticulous planning.

•

Don't rely solely on glossy hotel brochures to give you all of the information that you need. Remember that these brochures are simply marketing pieces and you still need to do your homework.

•

When you have narrowed down your hotels or regions, compare what travel critics from books and magazines have to say about specific properties.

•

At check-in, remind the hotel attendant that you are on your honeymoon. You may get a complimentary bottle of champagne or be upgraded to an especially private corner room or suite.

Travel Agent Tips

If you don't have the time or interest to plan it yourself, hand it over to a pro. Find a travel agent you can trust or who has been recommended by other honeymooners.

•

Agents have traveled to many honeymoon destinations. Just be wary of them dictating properties to you that they may have a vested interest in because they get kickbacks or special treatment.

•

Take your travel agent's emergency contact number with you on your honeymoon, just in case any complications arise.

•

Follow up with your travel agent to make sure he or she booked your flight tickets and hotel.

Budget Honeymoon Destinations

Consider a "couples-only" resort where everyone there will be in love and showing it! Plus, most activities at those types of resorts revolve around romance, and many offer great package deals.

•

Go to an all-inclusive resort where you pay one flat fee up front, so there will be no surprises at checkout. Most offer accommodations, meals, activities, drinks, and even honeymoon goodies for one fixed price.

•

Seek out a spot that is not viewed as a typical honeymoon destination such as Costa Rica, domestic bed and breakfasts, a European cooking school class in Italy, or a national park such as Yosemite or the Grand Canyon.

•

Hawaii is a super destination if you want to feel exotic yet remain in the United States. The Hawaiians love honeymooners and will demonstrate their aloha spirit time and again.

•

Europe in low season and by rail from country to country works very well on a budget. Use the *Let's Go* budget travel books, and purchase a Eurail pass to prepay for your travel while there.

•

South America and Mexico are also popular honeymoon destinations, especially when the U.S. dollar is strong.

●

Walt Disney World in Florida offers fun and discounted packages if you do your homework.

Daring, Unconventional, or Off-the-Beaten-Path Budget Destinations

Head to the Poconos for an inexpensive, romantic, and fun honeymoon. Many hotels offer heart-shaped bathtubs, private swimming pools, and fireplaces in the rooms, and the prices are truly out of this world.

●

Las Vegas is very doable on budget, and if you are lucky in the casinos, your honeymoon may pay for itself!

●

For total affordable privacy and some do-it-yourself expectations, how about renting a houseboat? Call your local visitors' bureau and ask for names of marinas and agencies that handle such rentals.

●

Borrow or rent an RV and drive around the country. Maybe you have generous relatives or friends who will let you convert their RV into your own honeymoon love nest. Chill champagne in the refrigerator daily and enjoy!

●

If you get married in the United States, staying domestic and driving instead of flying is a good, frugal alternative. How about combining sightseeing major landmarks and hitting romantic bed and breakfasts or inexpensive hotels along the way?

●

Rent a private cabin in the woods, or go camping to get away from it all.

Honeymoon Money and Personal Contacts

Get travelers' checks for your trip instead of carrying lots of cash or using credit cards. If you are unable to pay off your credit cards in full, the high interest rates will add significantly to the cost of your honeymoon.

●

Make photocopies of your tickets, passports, travelers' check receipts, and any emergency phone numbers or other information you may need. Take these with you on your trip, in a separate place from the originals.

•

Find a friend or relative who wants to give you their frequent-flyer miles as a wedding gift. Your honeymoon airfare will then be free.

•

See if you or your parents have a friend who has a second home, time-share, or other location you could borrow for your honeymoon. They could loan you the location as your wedding gift.

Travel Times and Transportation Tips

Look into hotel and car rental discounts to see which may apply based on your frequent-flyer airline account.

My advice to honeymooners on a budget? Try to get a free airline upgrade. Here's how: Be sure to bring your bouquet with you to the airport if you are flying somewhere for your honeymoon. The bridal bouquet alone can assist in getting you upgrades or at least complimentary champagne on the flight. It did for me!

—*Kate L., Atlanta, GA*

- -

If your wedding date permits or if you choose to postpone your honeymoon until a few months after the wedding, plan to travel during your destination's off or low season for cheaper rates. Seasonal discounts are not offered everywhere and differ by destination, so consult your hotel and plan your honeymoon travel accordingly. Many honeymoon destinations cost at least 50 percent less during off season.

- - - - - - - - - - - - - - - - - -

Super Duper Deal

If you are traveling by air, fly on off-peak days of the week—that is, Sunday through Wednesday.

- -

Have your honeymoon in the city where you were married, and save up for a bigger trip that is lengthier and costlier at a later date when your budget allows.

Frugal Freebie

Use frequent-flyer miles to fly away for your honeymoon. They are free and offer great flexibility (except for high-season blackout dates that may apply).

Cutting Costs on Hotel Arrangements

Whenever you book a hotel (or car rental), ask for all possible discounts. For example, check to see if they take the Entertainment card; have any promotions related to Diners Club, Visa, or another credit card; offer any frequent-flyer-mile deals; or give student, AAA, military, or government discounts or reduced honeymoon rates.

•

Read the fine print when booking any hotel's honeymoon package. Often, the added perks, such as airport transfers, champagne, and hotel robes, wind up costing more than if you just booked directly with the hotel and paid separately for the specific extras that you really want.

•

Ask if any meals, such as continental breakfast, are included with your hotel room.

•

Don't worry about booking the honeymoon suite—or any suite, for that matter. You often pay for lots more than you really need.

One of our wedding guests was a manager at an upscale hotel. I was friendly with his daughter who was also going to be attending the wedding and was asking me about what kinds of things were on our wish list for wedding gifts. I hinted to her that we were seeking wedding night locations and had basically blown our wad on the honeymoon. For our wedding gift, her father gave us our wedding night in a gorgeous suite in the hotel, complete with 360-degree panoramic view of the city and champagne to boot!

—*Carol M., St. Louis, MO*

Avoid minibar temptations and instead stock your in-room fridge with beverages and snacks from a nearby grocery or convenience store. They'll cost significantly less!

•

If you are unhappy with your room, speak up immediately. Where you sleep (and play!) makes a lot of difference in the mood and tone of your honeymoon.

•

Honeymoon disasters have been known to occur. If you experience one, document what happens, speak to managers, remind them you are honeymooners, and write letters after-the-fact if necessary. Just be sure to keep your sense of humor. These experiences make for great stories!

The Honeymoon Survey

Ask yourself some of these questions to help decide where you want to go and what you are willing to spend on your honeymoon:

1. What is your budget for this trip? Then add 10 percent for a cushion.
2. Do you like lots of other people around, or do you prefer to be isolated?
3. Do you like adventure and the outdoors or prefer a quiet escape?
4. Do you have different interests and vacation goals?

5. Do you want to plan your trip together or let one of you do most of the planning?

6. Do you want to use a travel agent?

Q. *We basically have no money left over in our budget to pay for our honeymoon. We've heard about registering at travel agencies, but we're wondering if that is tacky.*

A. Registering for honeymoons and even cash toward a down payment on your future home is becoming more and more acceptable and common. Many guests recognize that finances may be tight for you, especially when you are paying for your own wedding. While some guests may be put off by your request, many will be happy to contribute to your honeymoon fund, especially if that is what you really want and need. Just be sure to have a registry of some items as well for those guests who want to go the more traditional route.

Afterword

I hope that *The Frugal Bride* has inspired you to apply some fun and creative ways to frugally plan your wedding. Throughout the process, just keep your sense of humor, try to enjoy it all and not let it overwhelm you too much, and always look for ways to shave off some extra dollars while preserving your wedding vision. Rob dollars from one aspect of your celebration that you may have scrimped on and put the money toward another if need be. Just remember: You can have a frugal wedding without looking cheap. Creative planning and careful research can turn a few-thousand-dollar wedding into a million bucks. I wish you a wonderful beginning together and a happily ever after.

Bargain Web Sites, Magazines, and Other Publications

The references here are meant to guide you to other helpful budget idea sources. You do not need to subscribe to wedding magazines. Much of the information is redundant, and you can skim them at bookstores or bridal salons. But if you choose to, subscribe for an entire year as opposed to buying them monthly. You'll save over half the cover price in most cases. Also, don't feel compelled to buy any or all of the books listed here. Skim the referenced chapters at the bookstore or your local library, and bring a notebook to jot down ideas.

Web Sites

Check out these as a place to start, and by all means use your own search engine (yahoo.com, google.com, askjeeves.com, altavista.com, AOL, Internet Explorer, etc.) for other leads. There are literally hundreds of thousands of wedding sites and items out there to be found. Limit your searches to include the word *budget*

and see what you discover. Here are a few of my favorites to get you started:

Wedding Planning Web Sites with Budget Areas

www.angelfire.com Offers a frugal bride area.

www.bwedd.com A budget wedding newsletter put out biweekly by a former bride with a knack for budgeting.

www.modernbride.com Has an "All About Budget" section.

www.theknot.com Includes a great area dedicated to budget as well as a comprehensive and exhaustive creative budgeter that allows you to input your information and toggle with numbers to see where you can cut and add.

www.trumpmoon.ltd.uk

www.ultimatewedding.com Contains several articles pertaining to budget.

www.windsorpeak.com Denise and Alan Field's Web site. Go to the "Bridal Bargains" area for updates and information.

You may also want to check out these sites:

www.beverlyclark.com
www.blisszine.com
www.bridalplanner.com

www.brideandgroom.com

www.latinabride.com

www.marthastewart.com You can even purchase back issues of her wedding magazine online.

www.premierbride.com

www.todaysbride.com

www.weddingbells.com

www.weddinglinksgalore.com

Destination Weddings

www.bluehawaiiweddings.com Offers Hawaiian budget weddings information, or call (808) 883-2583.

www.sandals.com or 888-SANDALS

www.thebahamas.com

www.towd.com Tourism Offices Worldwide

Contact Information to Check On Your Vendor's Track Record

The Association of Bridal Consultants: Call (860) 355-0464 or send an e-mail to bridalassn@aol.com.

The Better Business Bureau: www.betterbusiness bureau.com offers phone numbers of your local office.

Your local Chamber of Commerce: www.chamber ofcommerce.com for the World Chamber of Commerce Directory, or check you local white pages.

Wedding Magazines

Check out www.magazinecity.net for discounts on subscriptions.

Bridal Guide

Bride Again

Bride's

Brides and Setting Up Home
Modern Bride

Wedding Pages

Other Publications

Here are a few other publications that focus on budget. Also check out general wedding books and browse their budget chapters.

The Ultimate Wedding Idea Book: 1,001 Creative Ideas to Make Your Wedding Fun, Romantic, & Memorable, by Cynthia C. Muchnick (Prima Publishing, 2000). Budget ideas are scattered throughout, and a chapter is dedicated to budgetary concerns.

How to Have an Elegant Wedding for $5,000 or Less, by Jan Wilson and Beth Wilson Hickman (Prima Publishing, 1999). The title says it all!

Bridal Bargains, by Denise and Alan Fields (Windsor Peak Press, 2000). Thick, dense, and chock full of consumer information—a bit overwhelming and tedious, but that's a bit like wedding planning, isn't it?

The Knot's Complete Guide to Weddings in the Real World, by Carley Roney (Bantam Books, 1998). A brief budget chapter and other points sprinkled throughout. Also, a paper budget planner is located in the appendix with suggested percentages of how much you should spend on each wedding aspect.

The Cheapskate's Guide to Weddings and Honeymoons: Doing It Right Without Spending a Fortune, by David W. Shaw. (Citadel Press, 1996). A bit dated and not too user friendly, but does contain some helpful budget ideas.

Weddings for Dummies, by Marcy Blum and Laura Fisher Kaiser (IDG Books, 1997). A special chapter is dedicated to "The Ten Tricks of Saving Money."

Creative Wedding Florals You Can Make, by Terry L. Rye (Betterway Books, 2000). This series offers other titles, too, such as *Creative Wedding Keepsakes You Can Make,* by Terry L. Rye and Laurel Tudor (Betterway Books, 2001) and *Creative Decorations You can Make,* by Teresa Nelson (Betterway Books, 1998) with fully illustrated step-by-step instructions on how to do these things yourself.

The Complete Idiot's Guide to the Perfect Wedding, by Teddy Lenderman and Gerard J. Monaghan (Alpha Books, 2000). Contains a chapter titled "Making the Most of Your Dollars."

The Budget Wedding Sourcebook, by Madeline Barillo (McGraw-Hill, 2000). Practical, organized and serves as a good budget planner, too.

How to Buy a Diamond, by Fred Cuellar (Sourcebooks, 2000). Debunks all of your diamond myths and provides excellent questions to ask jewelers.

How to Have a Big Wedding on a Small Budget, by Diane Warner (Betterway Books, 1997).

1001 Ways to Save Money . . . and Still Have a Dazzling Wedding, by Sharon Naylor (McGraw-Hill, 2001).

Priceless Weddings for Under $5000, by Kathleen Kennedy (Three Rivers Press, 2000).

The Perfect Wedding (Harper Collins, 1997) and *The Perfect Wedding Reception,* (Harper Resource, 2000) both by Maria McBride-Mellenger. These books offer gorgeous images and stunning ideas for classy wedding touches. You can find ways to pare down the high-end images into affordable solutions of your own.

The Beverly Clark Series, including *Weddings: A Celebration.* A beautiful coffee table book by Beverly Clark (Wilshire Publications, 1996), with classic images and ideas for an unforgettable wedding.

The New Book of Wedding Etiquette, by Kim Shaw (Prima Publishing, 2001). Covers all of your modern etiquette concerns.

Discount Retail Outlets and Registry Information

David's Bridal: (888) 480-BRIDE or www.davidsbridal.com. With currently 130 stores nationwide and more opening each week, David's even has an annual "$99.00 sale" during which selected gowns are significantly marked down. Call to find out your nearest store and to schedule an appointment.

Filene's Basement in Boston and New York has annual gown sales. Call (800) 427-4337.

Saturdays at New York trunk shows offer steals and deals. Ask around if you happen to be in town!

Bargain Stationary and Personalized Items

www.amazinginvitations.com: Or (478) 784-9247. Provides a wide assortment of do-it-yourself wedding card stock that you can print out at home.

The American Stationery Company, Inc.: (800) 822-2577 or www.americanstationery.com. This catalog offers good prices on many stationery products (excluding wedding invitations). They have some cute personalized bridesmaid or groomsman gift ideas, too.

Ann's Bridal Boutique: (215) 887-1089 or www.annsbridal.com. A huge resource spot for budget bargains in stationery and invitations.

www.finestationery.com: Also call (888) 808-FINE. A comprehensive Web site broken down by prices, products, and companies.

www.invitations4less.com: Offers 25 percent off retail prices.

The Personal Touch: (800) 733-6313 or www.thepersonaltouch.com. Bargain stationery for thank-you notes, invitations, printer card stock, and so forth. Also has fun wedding "Memoirs" such as personalized champagne flutes, pillowcases, and wedding video storage boxes. Join their buyers club to save 10 percent off on all orders.

www.theamericanwedding.com: Discount wedding invites and accessories.

www.thebusybride.com: An online listing of all catalogs so you can see them. Also, catalog prices are discounted 25 to 35 percent if ordered online.

 www.thingsremembered.com: Receive up to 20 percent off for online orders.

Registry

Discount China Registry

Michael C. Fina: (800) 288-FINA

Ross-Simons: (800) 458-4545

Department Stores and Off-the-Beaten-Path Ideas for Registering

Not all these stores may be in your area; call the 800 numbers (from within the United States) to find a store near you. All Web sites listed have a gift and/or bridal registry area.

Bed Bath & Beyond: www.bedbathandbeyond.com or (800) 462-3966

Bloomingdale's:
www.bloomingdales.weddingchannel.com

Crate & Barrel: www.crateandbarrel.com or (800) 967-6696

Eddie Bauer Home Store: www.eddiebauer.com

Filene's: www.filenes.com or (800) 4-BRIDES

The Home Depot: (800) 553-3199

Ikea: www.ikea-usa.com

JCPenney: www.jcpenney.com or (800) 222-6161

Linens-N-Things: www.lnt.com or (877) 568-9333 (nationwide gift registry). By the way, their guarantee is "If you find a lower price on the same item anywhere, even on sale, we'll match it."

Macy's: www.macys.com or (800) BUY-MACY

Neiman-Marcus: www.neimanmarcus.com or (888) 888-4757

Pier One Imports: www.pierone.com

Pottery Barn: www.potterybarn.com or (888) 779-5176

Recreational Equipment, Inc. (REI): www.rei.com or (800) 426-4840

Robinson's May: www.robinsonsmay.com or (800) 445-9959

Sears: www.sears.com or (800) 697-3277

Service Merchandise: www.servicemerchandise.com or (888) 764-4387

Target Club Wed: www.target.com or (800) 888-WEDD or 888-304-4000, option 2

Williams-Sonoma: www.williams-sonoma.com or (877) 812-6235

Bargain Contact Information for Other Wedding Services

Inexpensive Favors and Novelties

The Beverly Clark Collection: (800) 888-6866

The Oriental Trading Company: (800) 875-8480 or www.oriental.com

Bargain Travel Web Sites and Contact Information

Bargain Locations

The Bahamas: www.thebahamas.com

Ceasar's Poconos: (800) 233-4141

Las Vegas Wedding Chapels: www.vegas.com/wedding/chapels.html or Las Vegas Tourism at (702) 735-1616

Sandals WeddingMoon packages: (888) SANDALS or www.sandals.com

Super Clubs: (800) 859-SUPER or www.superclubs.com

Walt Disney World: www.disney.com

Bargain Travel Agents, Airfare, and Tickets

Arthur Frommer's Bargain Traveler magazine

Best Fares magazine or www.BestFares.com

www.cheapfares.com

Cheap Seats: (800) MRCHEAP

Cheap Tickets: (800) 377-1000 or www.cheaptickets.com

The Consumer Reports Travel Newsletter

Council Travel: (800) 226-8624 or www.counciltravel.com

www.Expedia.com

www.hotwire.com: Specially negotiated "hot fares" for airline, hotels, and rental cars.

www.Priceline.com: Name your own ticket price and see if it works!

www.Travelocity.com

The Frugal Wedding Budgeter

Here is a general budgeter breaking down all areas of a wedding. Percentages and numbers provided are only averages based on a one-hundred-person wedding celebration. For smaller or larger affairs, you can guesstimate. I am reluctant to include a price range of costs in my wedding breakdown, since so many factors are personal and based on your own guest numbers, location, season, and budgetary constraints. So, I recommend you begin with this draft. Then, move to online budgeters, wedding software, or your own Excel or other spreadsheet program so that you can make changes accordingly. (The interactive budgeter at www.theknot.com works really well.) As you will discover, not all of these areas are applicable to all weddings. Add or edit what applies to yours.

Your Budget Goal $_____
(add 10% for additions you may not have considered)

	What You Are Willing to Spend	What You Actually Spent	Savings
Proposing			
Engagement ring			
Wedding rings			
Engagement Announcements			
Personal stationery for thank-you notes			
Save-the-date announcements and prewedding mailing (include postage)			
Wedding Invitations			
Postage			
RSVP cards			
Calligraphy or printer fees			

Wedding Programs			
Attire			
Bridal gown			
Bridal accessories			
Shoes and hose			
Garter			
Jewelry			
Veil			
Gloves			
Hair			
Makeup			
Manicure/pedicure			
Lingerie			
Alterations			
Groom			
Tuxedo			

	What You Are Willing to Spend	What You Actually Spent	Savings
Shoes			
Studs and cuff links			
Alterations			
Groomsmen			
Tuxedos or suits			
Shoes			
Studs and cuff links			
Alterations			
Bridesmaids			
Dresses			
Accessories			
Hair and makeup			
Alterations			
Ring bearer, flower girls, and junior bridesmaids			

Gifts for the Wedding Party and Help

Groomsmen gifts

Bridesmaid gifts

Gifts for your fiancé

Ring bearer, flower girl, and junior bridesmaids

Gifts for vendors or tips

Registry

Prenuptial Parties and Other Prewedding Costs

Showers—gifts for hosts

Bachelor/bachelorette parties—thank-you notes for hosts

Rehearsal dinner—thank-you notes for hosts and
possible costs to you both

Legal fees for prenuptial agreement

Location, Ceremony, and Site Fees

Ceremony fee

Site fee

	What You Are Willing to Spend	What You Actually Spent	Savings
Marriage license			
Guest book			
Officiant's fee and/or church donation			
Place cards			
Table cards			
Gratuity			
Valet or parking fees			
Accessorizing Your Ceremony			
Aisle runner			
Alter flowers			
Huppah			
Unity candle			
Goblets			

Miscellaneous decorations

Rented live/artificial plants

Supplemental lighting

Flowers, centerpieces, and decorations

Floral centerpieces

Alternative centerpieces

Candles, fabric, containers, mirrors, topiaries, potted plants, and balloons

Bride's bouquet(s)

Bridesmaid bouquets

Boutonnieres: groom, fathers, grandfathers, ring bearer, ushers, and other honorees

Corsages: mothers and grandmothers

Cake-decorating flowers

Flowers for hair, flower girl, aisle ways, pews, and so forth

	What You Are Willing to Spend	What You Actually Spent	Savings
Wedding Favors			
Per couple			
Per individual			
Centerpiece to be randomly designated to one guest per table			
The Help			
Officiant fees			
Wedding consultant fees			
Photographer costs			
Proofs			
Negatives			
Wedding/engagement portrait			
Your wedding album			
Mothers' albums			
Disposable cameras			

	What You Are Willing to Spend	What You Actually Spent	Savings
Videographer			
Extra copies of the video			
Music			
Ceremony			
Reception			
Overtime			
Band versus deejay			
Transportation			
For bride and groom arrival and departure			
For out-of-town guests to and from activity locations			
Catering			
Beverages			
Wine			
Champagne			

	What You Are Willing to Spend	What You Actually Spent	Savings
Nonalcoholic			
Bartender			
Open bar versus cash bar			
Corkage or pouring fees			
Coffee/coffee bar			
Ice			
Mixers			
Meal costs per head			
Appetizers and/or hors d'oeuvres per head or platter			
Dessert			
Cake			
Additional dessert buffet?			

Cutting fee if not in-house baker

Groom's cake

Tipping the help

Rental Items if Not Included in Site Fees

Tables

Chairs

Table linens

China

Napkins

Flatware

Serving dishes

Tent

Dance floor or other flooring

Delivery fees

Taxes

	What You Are Willing to Spend	What You Actually Spent	Savings
Wedding Insurance			
Honeymoon			
Wedding-night room			
All-inclusive or nightly			
Airfare			
Airport transportation			
Car rental			
Hotel room			
Meals			
Souvenirs			
Traveler's checks			
Trousseau (bride's clothing for honeymoon)			

Send Me Your Frugal Ideas!

If the ideas in this book have inspired you or if you have frugal wedding ideas to share, I want to know about them. Please send your submissions via e-mail to MarryMe123@aol.com, or fax them to (949) 644-4135. You may also visit my Web site at www.cynthiamuch-nick.com for information on new publications and how to contact me. Be sure to include your name, address, phone number, or e-mail address with your idea so that you can be contacted if your submission is included in any future books.

Index

About the Author

Cynthia C. Muchnick was born and raised in Marin County, California. She received a bachelor's degree in art history and political science at Stanford University, where she met her husband, Adam Muchnick. After completing college, Cindy moved to Chicago, where she began her career in college admissions at the University of Chicago. Cindy and her husband relocated to Florida; there she earned her master's degree in liberal studies, taught tenth grade history, and wrote her first book, *Will You Marry Me? The World's Most Romantic Proposals*, followed by *101 Ways to Pop the Question*.

Cindy is proud to be dubbed a wedding expert and engagement coach. She has appeared on dozens of talk shows and news stations including *Leeza, Sally Jesse Raphael, Donny & Marie, Fox News, Good Day LA, Good Day New York* and many others. She also worked as a columnist and spokesperson for *Honeymoon* magazine and currently freelances for *Coast Magazine*. Her educational publication, *The Best College Admission Essays*, is a how-to book for high school students going through the college essay–writing process. Her recent wedding book, *The Ultimate Wedding Idea Book: 1001 Ways to Make Your Wedding Fun,*

Romantic, and Memorable, has become a must-have for brides and is well received in the wedding and media community.

Still incurable romantics, Cindy and her husband are living happily ever after with their two sons in southern California. To get an insider's advice on weddings, to book the author as a motivational speaker, or to order signed copies of her books, send an e-mail to MarryMe123@aol.com, and visit her Web site at www.cynthiamuchnick.com.